HONKY

BY GREG KALLERES

D0167935

DRAMATISTS
PLAY SERVICE
INC.

HONKY received its world premiere at Urban Stages (Frances Hill, Artistic Director) in New York City on March 15, 2013. It was directed by Luke Harlan; the set design was by Roman Tatarowicz; the costume design was by Sarah Thea Swafford; the lighting design was by Miriam Nilofa Crowe; the sound design was by Brandon Wolcott; the projection design was by Caite Hevner; the production manager was Sean Hagerty; and the production stage manager was Brian D. Gold. The cast was as follows:

THOMAS HODGE..Anthony Gaskins
DAVIS TALLISON .... Philip Callen
PETER TRAMMEL...Dave Droxler
EMILIA HODGE .... Arie Bianca Thompson
ANDIE CHASTAIN ....Danielle Faitelson
DR. DRISCOLL ....Scott Barrow
KID 1 ....Chris Myers
KID 2 ....Reynaldo Piniella

CHARACTERS

THOMAS HODGE: 30s, black male.

DAVIS TALLISON: 40s-50s, white male.

PETER TRAMMEL: 30s, white male.

EMILIA HODGE: 30s, black female; Thomas' sister.

ANDIE CHASTAIN: 25-35, white female; Peter's fiancée.

DR. DRISCOLL: 35-60, white male.

KID 1: 18-30, black male.

KID 2: 18-30, black male.

WILSON: Played by Dr. Driscoll.

REPORTER: Played by Dr. Driscoll.

FREDERICK DOUGLASS: Played by Kid 1.

ABRAHAM LINCOLN: Played by Dr. Driscoll.

This play should be performed without an intermission.

hon·ky (Hông'ke.) n. offensive slang;
A disparaging term for a white person

HONKY

Scene 1

"Sky Max 16 Commercial"

A screen projection of a poor, black, American neighborhood. A soulful woman sings to a melodramatic hip-hop beat.

SOULFUL WOMAN. *(Offstage.)*
 Oh, yeaaaah … oooh, yeaaaaaah …
(A silhouette of two black kids dressed stereotypically "ghetto" strut toward each other and begin playing a badass game of one-on-one.)
 When life is hard out in the street
 It matters what is on your feet
 Reach for the sky.
(It's choreographed beautifully, like a dance. It's about more than basketball.)
 When ghetto's in your sole
 And it's kinda like *The Wire* on HBO
 Reach for the sky. Reach for the sky.
(Kid 1 shoots. Kid 2 blocks. Kid 1 goes down. Angry, Kid 1 removes his sneaker and aims it at Kid 2, like a gun! Kid 2 then pulls off his Sky Max 16 shoe — a dramatic light shines on it. He aims it at Kid 1, who realizes he's over-matched and raises his hands in defeat.)
 Reach for the skyyyyyyy!!
(The Sky Max 16 logo appears.)
BADASS ANNOUNCER. The new SKY MAX 16!
KID 2. 'Sup Now! *(Then breaking all coolness we hear:)*
LESS BADASS ANNOUNCER. Now available at all Footlocker locations! *(Lights out.)*

Scene 2

A nice office. Davis Tallison, white, sits confidently behind a desk, scrutinizing a wildly-colored basketball sneaker. Across sits Thomas Hodge, black.

DAVIS. So, are they going to stay these colors?

THOMAS. Well, yeah. That's kinda the design. *(He waits as Davis examines it more.)*

DAVIS. Would you wear these?

THOMAS. You mean…? Sure. I mean. What do you mean?

DAVIS. I mean would you wear them?

THOMAS. Well, I wouldn't design anything I wouldn't wear.

DAVIS. No, I understand that; pride in your work and I get that. But … would you?

THOMAS. *(With conviction.)* Yes.

DAVIS. See, I think it looks like a circus shoe.

THOMAS. You don't like it.

DAVIS. I can't think of a pair of pants that would go with them.

THOMAS. You said the same thing about the 16s.

DAVIS. Right. Well, the first question, the important one, is would *you* wear them? You say you would. The next question is, would *I*? And the truth is, I wouldn't wear them on a bet.

THOMAS. Well. With all due respect Mr. Tallison, they're not for you. *(This sparks something in Davis.)*

DAVIS. No? Who are they for, Thomas?

THOMAS. They're for, well, black kids. They're for black kids. That's our target. Urban youth; 14-24.

DAVIS. Ahh. That does exclude me, doesn't it? Guess my opinion doesn't carry much weight around here.

THOMAS. No, that's not — what I meant was —

DAVIS. They're for your people. Right? It's okay. That what you're saying?

THOMAS. *(Beat; cautious.)* I was hired to design shoes for the urban youth market. Sky Shoes … I'm saying, Sky Shoes is an urban — *primarily* — black brand.

DAVIS. Fair enough. Now, let me tell you why I was hired.

THOMAS. Mr. Tallison …

DAVIS. No, please. You don't get to go to all these boring positioning meetings that I do, so let me fill you in on our *position*. I was brought in last year because this company has a property. An unusual property. And currently it's not living up to its potential. You know why?

THOMAS. No.

DAVIS. Because for the last fifteen years, Sky has been selling to *your* people and *only* your people. Is it cool if I talk like this? I'm not making you uncomfortable — "*my* people," "*your* people" — I grew up in Chicago. Point is, these are facts, yes? *(Before Thomas can answer.)* Now, I won't bore you with numbers here, but we've found a large sub-segment of suburban white kids who literally won't wear anything, listen to anything, *say anything* unless it's been legitimized by blacks first.

THOMAS. Legitimized.

DAVIS. By the urban market.

THOMAS. We don't sell to suburban white kids.

DAVIS. This is what I'm telling you — we do now! But see, turns out they won't trust us to sell them anything. That is, *they*, being my people, won't trust *us*, being white people. But they'll trust *you*.

THOMAS. My people.

DAVIS. There's this incredible phenomenon called white guilt. Have you heard of this? These kids who live off of Mommy and Daddy with their trust funds and private schools; it's like Kryptonite! We did a whole focus group on it; I'll show you the video, it's fascinating. Anyway, we can use this guilt to outsell our competitors. How? Because we have what Nike does not.

THOMAS. What's that?

DAVIS. We're really black! *(Thomas just stares.)* So, yes. We market to African Americans. Why? Because they're the best salesmen we have! So, again, the first question is, would you wear them? The second question is … would I? *(Beat.)* I'll get back to you with more detailed feedback on the design later in the week. *(Davis goes back to work. Thomas takes this as his cue to leave … but then stops.)*

THOMAS. What about when it becomes shit?

DAVIS. What's that?

THOMAS. Illegitimate. Watered-down popular culture. "Whoot, there it is."

DAVIS. In ten years we sell the "Whoot, there it is" retro shoe.

THOMAS. That explains the ad for the 16s.

DAVIS. You don't like it.

THOMAS. I designed a basketball shoe. That ad has nothing to do with basketball.

DAVIS. We're not selling basketball; we're selling culture!

THOMAS. You're selling the ghetto. And that tag line? "'Sup now?" What is that?!

DAVIS. "'Sup now." It's like … "What's up now," except —

THOMAS. I know what it means!

DAVIS. Oh. I see. I'm the white guy right now. Is that it? Hm? I can see that look you're giving me. It's okay. You're right. I'm just a salesman. The 16s were your design. Your brilliance. Personally, I found them silly looking, but we've got black kids killing each other in the streets for those things! Now, white kids see that and they respect it. It's stupid, I agree, but they do. They're taking notice and we did that. How? By selling the ghetto!

THOMAS. You're serious.

DAVIS. Black kid shoots someone for a pair of our shoes, white kid says, "Now that's something *real*! Something *authentic*!" They want it because they don't understand it! We need our brand to be accepted by real *black* America so we can become *real* to the posers of *white* America! You wanna know how we beat Nike? Hm? When it's white kids killing for our shoes. Then we win.

THOMAS. You're talking about the kid who was shot. Because of our commercial.

DAVIS. Who knows why people do these things. It's ghetto shit. I'm from Chicago and I still don't understand it. The point is: perception. Kid gets shot, in the ghetto, his shoes are missing — happens to be our shoes.

THOMAS. Mr. Tallison … I love this company. Like every kid in the neighborhood, I developed an early obsession with sneakers. Sky Max 3s were my first pair. After that, I was hooked. Fetishized them. Sometimes I'd hardly ever wear 'em. I'd just look at 'em. Feel 'em. Smell 'em. To this day, the smell of leather on a brand new shoe is the closest thing to true happiness I know. And every year, the new Sky shoe would come out in February, just before spring. It was the only thing kids from my street — "my people" — could talk about. And the only time a kid got hurt was when he scuffed someone's shit up. We loved Sky because it made no apologies. It was a black shoe for black people. And we saw a white kid wearing

10

'em, he better be able to back his shit up on the court or he was gonna get his ass beat. There was a purity to it. *(Beat.)* The kid who was killed? That was my little cousin. So, I'm sorry, but I don't quite share your enthusiasm for edging out the competition. You'll have my resignation by the end of the week. *(Thomas turns to the door.)*
DAVIS. Tom! Thomas! *(Thomas stops. Davis struggles.)* Is that...? Jesus, I'm ... obviously, I wouldn't have ... This country, Thomas ... and I'll tell you, there are things, like this, you see it day in and day out; violence and the divisions and a system that just, frankly ... *(Then empathy.)* My wife killed herself.
THOMAS. *(Confused beat.)* Excuse me?
DAVIS. That's right. Bottle of sleeping pills. Not a lot of people know that. First she stopped talking. Then she wouldn't leave her room. Started calling me by my middle name, Allen, which she only used when she was mad at me. One morning I walked in and ... well, the whole thing is goddamn senseless. *(Awkward pause. Then, re: the shoes.)* Hey, look, you know what ... let me take another look at these.
THOMAS. I'm sorry, I don't understand ...
DAVIS. You were right with the 16s, I have no reason to doubt you now. And I want you with me on this one, Thomas. What do you say?
THOMAS. *(Beat.)* Whoot, there it is. *(Lights out.)*

Scene 3

A therapist's office. Peter, white, sits across from Emilia, black. This is their first meeting and he's nervous.

Long pause as Peter fidgets, awkwardly.

PETER. I'm sorry, I don't really know what I'm supposed to say.
EMILIA. That's alright. Why don't you tell me what's on your mind.
PETER. *(Beat.)* Getting married soon.
EMILIA. Congratulations.
PETER. Thank you, she's very white. *(Awkward beat.)* I don't know why I just said that. I don't mean white, like the distinction between the colors white or black. I mean, she's just very, you

know … *white*. This is sounding bad. I don't mean "white" like, "lynch you" white — and shit! I don't mean "lynch" as in…! Or even "you" as in — ! Jesus. How did I—? I didn't mean to make it a thing about, you know …

EMILIA. Okay.

PETER. Because the truth is, I'm totally color blind. And I don't mean that figuratively either. I mean, I don't see color. You should see my socks — totally integrated! *(Beat, careful.)* The point I'm making is that I'm getting married … to a woman … who is not a racist.

EMILIA. That's the point you're making.

PETER. It wasn't originally.

EMILIA. So, she's not a racist.

PETER. Or maybe she is! Who knows, right? I mean, they say everyone is kind of, you know, even if they don't think they are.

EMILIA. Does that include you?

PETER. Me?! Are you kidding?! My mom marched with Dr. King! Well, not technically. She overslept and missed the actual march. But she was a huge fan!

EMILIA. So, we've established that you, your fiancée and your mother are not racists.

PETER. *(Choosing words carefully.)* Right. Well. To say you're not racist is ignorant and ignorance is the very seed of racism. What I mean is, I don't hate someone because of the color of their skin or the slant of their eye. I don't mean "slant" as in … my point is, I like African Americans! *(Realizing this is stupid.)* But not just because they are so! I mean, I like some and I don't like some. Like I like some white people and hate some white people — like any race!

EMILIA. The Chinese?

PETER. Sure! Hate them too. And like them! My point is, I don't hate *because* they're Chinese. And I think that's what we're talking about here.

EMILIA. Is it?

PETER. Right? Exactly! "Is it?" And I didn't mean to imply that all racists are white either. I think racism is an equal-opportunity kind of thing. Hell, you could be a racist.

EMILIA. I could.

PETER. Of course! You can be anything you want! That's what's so great about this country! And I don't mean to say that all racists are bad people. Some are very good people! Good people who just don't know because they didn't have the money for the education.

My Aunt Judy? Total racist. But you can't blame her because she grew up poor, so it doesn't really count. And she's white! *(Chuckles.)* Well, of course she's white. *(Beat.)* Or she might not be! I didn't mean to imply that because I'm Caucasian she has to be Caucasian. It's very possible, not knowing me or my heritage, that she could be African American. Or Chinese. Or Asian! Not that all Chinese are Asian, obviously.

EMILIA. *(Correcting him.)* Not that all Asians are Chinese.

PETER. Right. Some are Japanese. Korean. Oriental.

EMILIA. "Oriental" is not politically correct.

PETER. Well, we can't blame them for that; it's probably just a culture thing. I've written papers about this exact thing.

EMILIA. You have?

PETER. One. Yeah. In college. Same thing we're talking about.

EMILIA. And what is that again?

PETER. *(False modesty, comfort.)* Oh, you know. This whole thing we're discussing. This whole silly race thing. It was actually in the school chronicle. Not a big deal really but the piece was very popular among the African American students. And Caucasians. All of them.

EMILIA. Hispanics?

PETER. Yes. They loved it too.

EMILIA. And the Asians?

PETER. Not a lot of Chinese at my school. Point is, I've written about this and I have a lot of strong feelings and I think that's kind of what we're both saying here. *(Long awkward pause. Peter forces a smile, trying to look comfortable.)*

EMILIA. Peter ... before you came here today, did you know that I was black?

PETER. *(Innocent.)* Uh ... why do you ask?

EMILIA. Because you seem a tad uncomfortable with it.

PETER. *(Pretending to be floored.)* ... What???

EMILIA. And, as a therapist, I want you feeling comfortable. If my being black keeps you from being honest or comfortable, I could refer you to another therapist. *(Peter fidgets, trying to decide if he should take the out she's offered.)*

PETER. Well, I'm just ... The idea that you think — because I know the people you're talking about and ... Whew! Man. I ... This is ... Okay! Okay! I'm going to be honest here. When I walked in and saw that you were not some whitey-white, stuck-up,

Dr. Phil yuppie, I was so relieved. I gotta tell you, I can't wait to tell you my problems and stuff.

EMILIA. Okay. Why don't you tell me why you came to see me today.

PETER. *(Pause, coming clean.)* A kid was murdered for a pair of shoes and I think it's because of a commercial I wrote.

EMILIA. Sky Shoes. You wrote that ad? "'Sup now?"

PETER. *(Sheepish, trying to joke.)* Not too much. How are you? *(Lights out.)*

Scene 4

A bedroom. Andie does her evening stretching exercises as she speaks to someone offstage.

ANDIE. Oh, my parents called! They want to know what we're doing for the holiday weekend. I said I'd ask you but I think they want us to go up to Connecticut. They're gonna have the Brennans up. Remember the Brennans? Mr. Brennan's the one who always smells like mayonnaise. Apparently, they're family now! For the past few months my parents keep referring to them as Aunt and Uncle for some reason. Oh, that reminds me, I haven't told you this yet because my therapist and I are still kind of working it out, but I'm pretty sure I have a repressed memory of Mr. Brennan touching me as a kid. *(Peter emerges from the bathroom.)* I mean, it's repressed, so you never know for sure, but I get a queasy, after-school special type of feeling around him. And whenever he sees me in a bathing suit he gives me this very specific sort of, "Whoa, I think I may have molested you once," kind of look. Plus when I go to sleep in my old house, I have this immediate craving for a turkey sandwich. You know. Turkey? Mayo? Probably means nothing but my therapist is gonna think about it. So, anyway, Mom asked the other day if we wanted Mr. Brennan to do our wedding service because he's some sort of judge and I was like, "Are you kidding?" Can you see us up there saying our vows and I suddenly smell Miracle Whip and have a panic attack?! *(Peter sits on the bed to get dressed.)*

PETER. I saw that woman today.

ANDIE. Oh good! How was it?

PETER. She was nice.

ANDIE. Don't be discouraged if you don't like her right away. It's normal. It took me four years to like my therapist.

PETER. I like her.

ANDIE. What did she say about the shooting? Did she tell you it's not your fault, or did she do that thing where she makes you figure it out on your own?

PETER. There was a witness.

ANDIE. In her office?

PETER. No, to the shooting. Just came forward. Saw the whole thing. Know what the kid said before he shot him? "'Sup now?"

ANDIE. *(Proud.)* Honey, that's your line! *(Realizing.)* I didn't mean that. Obviously. Hey, honey? It is not your fault. People kill. They buy guns and they shoot and they kill. It has nothing to do with you or your commercial. It's a testament to your talent that you even got people to buy those things in the first place! *(Off his look.)* Well, Peter, they're ugly shoes. What pants would even go with those things? *(She exits to the bathroom. We hear her brushing her teeth in the bathroom. Offstage.)* Killing people for shoes. What is this, the '80s? *(She pops her head out.)* Can you imagine women killing each other for shoes?! Not to be, you know, but can you?! Of course, I say that but Peg was wearing the hottest pair of Manolos the other day at lunch and I considered shooting her in the face myself! *(Pointing her finger.)* 'Sup now, BITCH! Pow! *(Lights out.)*

Scene 5

Emilia sits at her desk when Thomas bursts though the door —

THOMAS. Reach for the skyyyy!

EMILIA. Thomas — ?!

THOMAS. Reach for the sky mothafuckaaaas!!!

EMILIA. What are you doing? I have patients outside — !

THOMAS. I need you to look at my ass!

EMILIA. What?

THOMAS. Quickly! Look at my ass!

EMILIA. Okay! Okay! *(She bends down and looks.)*

THOMAS. Are you looking?

EMILIA. Yes!

THOMAS. You sure?

EMILIA. I'm looking!

THOMAS. Do you see a white man's dick in there anywhere?!

EMILIA. Jesus, Thomas!

THOMAS. I'm a bitch, Em! I'm a white man's bitch!

EMILIA. Okay, calm down …

THOMAS. I knew it'd take a toll! Growin' up around all those rich white people takes a toll. It takes a fuckin' toll!

EMILIA. Okay …

THOMAS. I knew eventually I'd be getting fucked by Clay Aiken, Coldplay, and *Downton Abbey*! I'd wake up in a cold sweat needing to buy some $600 Nottingham Wall Sconce from Pottery Barn!

EMILIA. You said that sconce gave your place a nice classic feel.

THOMAS. Damn right it's a nice classic feel! It's also an elegant way to disguise the lack of furniture in that part of the room — but you're missing the point!!

EMILIA. And that is?

THOMAS. This is not what black people talk about!!

EMILIA. Not this again. What are we supposed to talk about, Thomas?

THOMAS. I don't know — black shit!

EMILIA. Black shit.

THOMAS. Black shit that black people talk about, and you and I have been living around whitey so long we don't know how to do it anymore!

EMILIA. Don't say whitey.

THOMAS. Why, am I insulting you?

EMILIA. It's base.

THOMAS. What about nigger? Is that "base"? Because that's what my boss called me today!

EMILIA. Your boss called you — ??

THOMAS. Not as in the *word*, no. But with his eyes, you know? His tone, his whole: "It's cool, I'm from Chicago" — I mean, did I miss something? What the fuck happened in Chicago?! Shit, Emilia, I'm black! I can say "whitey" whenever I want!

EMILIA. You've earned it, huh?

16

THOMAS. Damn right; my heritage!

EMILIA. Your heritage is Rumson, New Jersey. And I don't think Bob Gammons would like you calling him whitey.

THOMAS. Bob Gammons?! Fuck Bob Gammons!

EMILIA. Fuck Bob Gammons?

THOMAS. Fuck him!

EMILIA. That's nice Thomas! He was like an uncle!

THOMAS. Fuck him! And fuck whitey!!

EMILIA. *(Gesturing to the door.)* Shhh! Thomas!

THOMAS. *(To the door.)* Whitey! Whitey! Cracker! Honky! White … trash … K K … *(Struggles for breath.)* I can't breathe …

EMILIA. Sit down.

THOMAS. I'm having … a …

EMILIA. You're having a panic attack. Sit down.

THOMAS. Panic? I'm having a damn … heart attack!

EMILIA. Shhh. Sit down. You're hyperventilating. Listen to me. Okay? Breathe in. Breathe out. Slow. Breathe in. Good. Out. *(He rests his head on her shoulder.)* Used to do that as a kid. Remember? Scared the hell out of Mom and Dad. Never knew what you were so nervous about. *(She gets some pills from a drawer.)* Take this. *(She exits to the bathroom.)*

THOMAS. Black people don't hyperventilate!

EMILIA. *(Offstage.)* It's an anxiety attack!

THOMAS. They don't have anxiety attacks neither! *(She emerges with water.)*

EMILIA. You'd be surprised.

THOMAS. Oh yeah? How many black patients do you have? *(He takes a drink, lays his head back.)* I made a work of art, and they turned it into a rap video.

EMILIA. I know.

THOMAS. I shoulda quit. I shoulda left the moment they hired that white motherfucker to sell our shoes!

EMILIA. Thomas …

THOMAS. I'm not gonna let that shit happen to the 17s, Em. It's the best thing I've ever done and I won't let another Charley Cross get shot because I let them put my shoes on thugs instead of black people!

EMILIA. C'mon, Thomas. Make it sound like you knew the kid.

THOMAS. *(Smiles devilishly.)* Yeah, well … I told Tallison he was my cousin.

EMILIA. You what??

THOMAS. You should've seen his face. And I thought he couldn't get any whiter.

EMILIA. You lied to your boss?

THOMAS. *(Proud.)* Yeah and he believed me. *(Then realizing.)* So fuck him for thinking all black people know each other! And then he comes back to me with this whole, "It's okay, my wife killed herself" bullshit!

EMILIA. His wife?

THOMAS. I know, right? Why you gotta top my shit!? Why does your wife's suicide beat my cousin's murder!?

EMILIA. He wasn't your cousin!

THOMAS. Yeah, but he didn't know that!!

EMILIA. Well, he didn't die because of his shoes or some stupid commercial and you know it.

THOMAS. They quoted the ad, Emilia.

EMILIA. The kid was a gangbanger!

THOMAS. And so he deserved to die?!

EMILIA. Will you cut that shit out!! Damn! I'm on your side! *(She calms, collects.)* Look, I know you feel this guilt. This ... conflict. Somehow you got it in your head that because you grew up with money and education you're not black enough. But getting yourself shot doesn't make you black, it makes you stupid.

THOMAS. Oh, so he was stupid too!

EMILIA. You see this? You talk about how offended you are at this commercial. Its portrayal of black ghetto youth as aspirational, and yet you defend the lifestyle. It's just like when we were kids. And you were always playin' ball with those gangsters from the neighborhood over —

THOMAS. You mean my friends?!

EMILIA. Friends?! You'd come home crying every time! All the shit they'd give you? Call you "rich boy," call you "white" — "honky!" Make fun of how you dressed, how you talked. And next day, sure enough, you'd go back for more.

THOMAS. Don't do that, alright? Don't analyze me like you do your white people.

EMILIA. That's the difference between us, Thomas. They are not "white people" to me. They're people with problems.

THOMAS. And you think they just see you as their doctor.

EMILIA. How else would they see me, Thomas?

THOMAS. No, see, they go home and they say, *(Imitating a white woman.)* "Jill! I'm seeing a new therapist, and you know what, she's

(Whispers.) black! Isn't that interesting? But she's so smart and articulate; you almost don't even think about it."

EMILIA. Does everything have to be so heavy?! Is that what talking about "black shit" is? Mining for the diabolical subtext? Stereotypical conversations about the white man keeping us down? You don't seem down, Thomas!

THOMAS. I'm gonna find him, Em. I'm gonna find that black-ass motherfucker who wrote that ad …

EMILIA. Thomas, what makes you think he's black?

THOMAS. I'm not kidding. At the 16 party tomorrow night, I'ma walk up to him, take him outside and I'ma show his ass wa'sup now! *(Lights out.)*

Scene 6

Davis' office. Wilson sits across from Davis.

WILSON. Look, I don't want to take too much of your time with this, or make too much of it, so I'll try to keep this brief. It seems there have been comments around the office concerning your … insensitivity.

DAVIS. Insensitivity.

WILSON. Some people have made mention. Some of the minorities. Do you see what I'm saying?

DAVIS. No.

WILSON. They, that is, the people who have made mention, the minorities, they have made claims that you might be a little … well, insensitive.

DAVIS. Insensitive.

WILSON. Racially.

DAVIS. You're kidding.

WILSON. Let me make this clear, this is not me talking to you right now. This is the board. Unfortunately, my hands are tied. Complaints have been filed. Measures need to be taken. By me. On the record. I have to have this conversation with you.

DAVIS. You do?

WILSON. Well, the board does. Technically, I'm not even here.

DAVIS. I see.

WILSON. Look, obviously you've been through something. Your wife. And my God, I mean, my God. So, don't think anyone holds anything against you. But it has to be on the record that you have heard what I've said and that steps will be taken. So ... have you heard what I've said?

DAVIS. ... Yes.

WILSON. And will steps be taken?

DAVIS. I'm sorry, to do what?

WILSON. To be less ... To be more ... sensitive.

DAVIS. What exactly is it that I did wrong?

WILSON. No one is saying you did anything wrong. There are *things*, in the workplace, with *people*, certain situations in which one must exercise *caution*. The things one *says*, *how* they're said and, in turn, how they are *received*. Do you understand?

DAVIS. Did this come from Thomas Hodge?

WILSON. Who?

DAVIS. Then who said it?

WILSON. Well, it was more than one person.

DAVIS. How many?

WILSON. I can't tell you that.

DAVIS. Look, I'll guess a number and if you say nothing, I'll know it's a yes, okay? *(Beat.)* Okay?

WILSON. I was saying yes.

DAVIS. Oh. Good. Two?

WILSON. No.

DAVIS. Three? *(Beat.)* Three people?

WILSON. Sorry, I was thinking about something else. Look, this is a delicate time. And things are very, well, they're delicate. And the board just doesn't want *this* thing or anything *else* to get in the way of *that*.

DAVIS. Okay. So, what, you're telling me...?

WILSON. The *board* is telling you.

DAVIS. Telling me what?

WILSON. Our goals, expanding Sky Shoes, widening our demo, selling to Nike ... these things are the important things.

DAVIS. Let me get this straight: The board is concerned that Nike will back out if they hear that employees said I'm racist?

WILSON. Whoa! Hey! Okay. Let's keep the R-word out of it.

DAVIS. But isn't that what they're saying?

WILSON. Yes, but it's their word. We can't really use it.

DAVIS. *(Fed up.)* Look, I truly appreciate the opportunity you've given me here at Sky. But I've been in this industry for twenty years. I don't give a shit if someone is black, Arab, Chinese, or Martian. All I care about is who's buying what, where they live and what they can afford. That's not racism, it's marketing. You wanna talk about stereotypes? We pay a premium for them. They're called *demographics*. *Out there* it may be racist to say that poor black people like malt liquor, fried chicken, and McDonalds. But *in here*? It's just a Power Point presentation. So, if the board wants to fire me for doing the job they hired me to do, it would be good to know. Meanwhile, if you'll excuse me, I have a black shoe company to paint white. *(Davis exits.)*

WILSON. *(Discomfited.)* Yikes. *(Wilson writes it all down. Lights out.)*

Scene 7

Peter and Andie's apartment. Peter reads on his laptop as Andie sits on the floor working on wedding invitations.

ANDIE. Have you sent me your list yet?

PETER. Huh?

ANDIE. Your new invitation list. Did you email it to me? I haven't gotten it.

PETER. Yeah, I haven't sent it yet.

ANDIE. Okay; let me know when you send it.

PETER. *(Beat, short.)* Well, I'll just, you know, send it, and then you'll know.

ANDIE. I just wanna try to email it to my parents before they go to bed. I got mine down to one-fifty. Which is good, I think. Assuming twenty-five don't come, I think we're okay. If you can get yours down to like one-twenty, assuming fifteen don't come, we should be in pretty good shape. Unless they do come. Which I doubt, but I don't want to over-assume. Or under-assume. I guess I'm wondering how much assuming you think we can do, over all. *(Beat.)* Peter? Are you listening to me?

PETER. More people were killed.

ANDIE. For the shoes?

PETER. In the Congo. Six hundred deaths this week!

ANDIE. God.

PETER. Six hundred!

ANDIE. Horrible. What are Betty and Dell's kids' names?

PETER. August and Minnesota. This is genocide! It's genocide and it's like the country, we, because, what, I mean, we'll go where there's oil, right? But, hey, a good old fashioned holocaust?

ANDIE. AIDS too.

PETER. You're damn right, AIDS! Wait, what about AIDS?

ANDIE. In the Congo.

PETER. *Yes!* Right. And *rape!* Women over there, I mean, and I've read about this — it's like a national pastime! And what do we do? It's like because it's not here. Because it doesn't affect us — why are we inviting Betty and Dell's kids?

ANDIE. I'm assuming they won't come. How did they die?

PETER. Who?

ANDIE. The six hundred?

PETER. I don't know. I just read the headline. AOL's got a poll about it. I'm doing it. I'm fucking doing it!

ANDIE. You should!

PETER. *(Reading.)* "Do you think the US should help in the Congo?" Fuck. Yes. *(He hits a button on his computer.)*

ANDIE. Vote for me too.

PETER. Huh?

ANDIE. Vote for me.

PETER. You can only vote once per screenname.

ANDIE. Oh.

PETER. And you know why it is, don't you? And this is what kills me: It's because they're black! You know that, right? I mean, if this was a white, European nation we'd be over there in a heartbeat! But because African Americans have no power in this country, we just mail them food and a few pairs of jeans and be done with it.

ANDIE. Isn't our country run by an African American?

PETER. Right, well, one! *(A moment.)*

ANDIE. I was talking to Tshombe at work. He's the guy I was telling you about. The one from Zambia? He hates it when white people refer to normal black people as "African American."

PETER. *(Defensive, insecure.)* What do you mean?

ANDIE. Well, he's *African*, like *from* Africa, so for him it's annoying. I mentioned a book to him and said that the author was African American and he said, "Is he really?" You know, with this tone.

PETER. Who?

ANDIE. Tshombe.

PETER. No, the author. Who was it?

ANDIE. Oh. The guy who wrote *Another Country*.

PETER. Ralph Ellison.

ANDIE. No the other one.

PETER. Langston Hughes.

ANDIE. No, the other one. Anyway, Tshombe said, "Is he from Africa?" And I said, "I don't think so." And he said, "Then he's not African American. I'm African American. I'm from Zimbabwe."

PETER. Zambia.

ANDIE. I think it's Zimbabwe. Anyway, he doesn't like when white people refer to black people as African American because he is African. They're just … Americans.

PETER. *(Beat.)* I think I say "black" mostly.

ANDIE. Me too. *(Then.)* Unless I'm talking to a black person. *(Pause.)*

PETER. We don't know shit.

ANDIE. Totally.

PETER. No, I mean, we have our little, you know, but *out there*? There's shit happening! Important shit! And what do we know?

ANDIE. Are you talking about the Congo or black people?

PETER. Both! Syria!! I mean, look at us!

ANDIE. Syria?

PETER. Yes, fucking Syria, Haiti!! People are dying is my point! And we are so — sheltered! So — I mean — *you*?!

ANDIE. Me?

PETER. Well, yes, honey, you! You grew up, you had everything. Money, care, opportunity. A three hundred-person wedding?! You're living proof that the American dream is a congenital affectation!

ANDIE. That's not my fault.

PETER. But doesn't it bother you?

ANDIE. What?

PETER. This! Our whole thing! Don't you feel a little … you know …

ANDIE. What??

PETER. For this! All of this that we have!

ANDIE. We work; we have jobs.

PETER. But you have a job because you're educated and you're educated because you grew up in a wealthy, white family!!

ANDIE. What does being white have to do with it?

PETER. There's a plight! A struggle and a plight that you know nothing about because you were born the way you are!

ANDIE. I know the plight.

PETER. You don't know the plight!

ANDIE. Oh, and you know the plight?

PETER. Yes! I know — not all of it — but a lot of the plight, yes! My mom marched with Dr. King for Christ sake!

ANDIE. No, she didn't — !

PETER. Not next to him! Not literally! But she marched! As in "the march"! As in the idea! A movement!

ANDIE. Peter, just because you went to public high school doesn't make you Nelson Mandela.

PETER. I'm just saying, when I grew up, I was taught to feel a certain, you know, level of a kind of ...

ANDIE. Guilt?

PETER. Yes! Exactly! Guilt!

ANDIE. And that's good?

PETER. I think when you consider the plight, a smidgen of guilt is the least you can feel!

ANDIE. So because you're a neurotic mess, I should be too?

PETER. Neuro — ?? Is that what you've gleaned from this whole thing?! I'm talking about suffrage here! Plight!

ANDIE. Stop saying plight!

PETER. Struggle!

ANDIE. I think this is your struggle, not theirs.

PETER. Don't say "theirs" like they're a "they"! They are not a "they"!

ANDIE. Who are you talking about?!

PETER. Who are you talking about?!

ANDIE. Are you still in therapy?!

PETER. GOD, YOU ARE SO FUCKING WHITE!!!

(Lights out.)

Scene 8

A newscast. A reporter in the field.

REPORTER. Early this morning, in the quiet, suburban town of Greenwich, Connecticut, Felix Sanders, a white teenage boy, was shot in the leg for what appears to be his basketball shoes. A possible reaction to what occurred two weeks ago when an African American teen was shot and killed for the same brand of shoes: Sky Max 16s. This time, however, witnesses claim the crime was committed by a group of young white males. All of whom were wearing crooked baseball caps, extra-large shirts, and baggy jeans. Some of the clothes, they say, were *actually* being worn ... backwards. *(Lights out.)*

Scene 9

A subway car. Davis sits staring out when two black kids get on the train, laughing and being very loud.

KID 1. Nah, nah, nah, nigga; that movie was the shit!
KID 2. Nigga, whatchu smokin'?! That ending can suck my dick!
KID 1. What, you telling me, you sittin' there, gang a hard mothah-fuckahs come up to you — you ain't got no choice!
KID 2. Nah, I ain't takin' it like a bitch.
KID 1. Nigga! Five hard niggas! Whatchu gonna do?!
KID 2. Run.
KID 1. They catch up.
KID 2. I do what that guy did in the movie.
KID 1. Yo, daz cuz nigga had a knife, son!
KID 2. I'd have a knife!
KID 1. You ain't gotta knife now. Nah. Dat shit happens now, you gotta take it. Question is, after you take they shit ...

DAVIS. Excuse me ...

KID 2. I'd get a damn gun, son, blow the nigga's joints off.

DAVIS. Excuse me ...

KID 1. Nigga, you lie.

DAVIS. Excuse me!

KID 1. *What?!*

DAVIS. Wondering if you wouldn't mind keeping it down.

KID 1. Last I checked, it was a free country.

DAVIS. Freedom doesn't mean we can't express a little courtesy.

KID 2. My man, how we not being "courteous"?

DAVIS. Well, frankly, you're being very loud. And there are children, and you're using words like, "shit" and "nigger" ... *(Suddenly the tone changes.)*

KID 1. What did you just say mothafuckah?!?

DAVIS. Nothing; I was repeating what you said.

KID 2. Nah, my man called us nigger!

DAVIS. What? No! I said — *you* said —

KID 1. What?!

DAVIS. You called him ...

KID 2. What?!

DAVIS. Nigger.

KID 2. He said it again, nigga!

DAVIS. You just said it again!

KID 1. What?

DAVIS. Uh — he — nigger!

KID 2. Nigga-what-nigga!?!?

DAVIS. Listen, let's take the N-word out of the conversation.

KID 1. I think that'd be wise for you. *(Kids look threatening.)*

DAVIS. Obviously, I've said something to offend you and I apologize. It's been a very bad day. Plus, the truth is, my wife ... *(Stops himself.)* Point is, I think I can clear this up. I see you're wearing Sky shoes!

KID 2. What about my shoes, bitch?

DAVIS. I'm the president of the company.

KID 1. You're kidding.

DAVIS. Well, I'm on probation, but for all practical purposes ... *(He pulls a card from his pocket.)* Here, now, you take that to any Footlocker retailer, they'll give you a free pair.

KID 2. Do I get one? I want one.

DAVIS. Well, I only have the one with me.

KID 1. Why you givin' me this?

KID 2. I think he was scared.

DAVIS. No. I just don't want any trouble.

KID 2. What did you think we was gonna do?

DAVIS. Nothing.

KID 2. Damn, man. Give the racist his damn card back.

KID 1. Easy for you to say! You didn't get one!

KID 2. Fine, nigga, keep it! Uncle Tom mothafuckah.

KID 1. *(Looks at Kid 2, guilty.)* Damn. *(He throws the card back at him.)* Racist mothahfuckah. *(The kids exit the car, leaving Davis alone. Lights out.)*

Scene 10

Dr. Driscoll's office. Davis listens, reluctantly, as Dr. Driscoll points to a map of the human brain.

DR. DRISCOLL. Driscotol works to isolate a small portion of the occipital lobe and numbs it, just slightly. This area here. Not coincidentally, it's the occipital lobe that is responsible for our memory and vision. Damage to this area can cause amnesia, hallucinations and what is referred to as "color agnosia." Loss of color. The drug itself was discovered after examining the head wound of a KKK Grand Wizard, who, while re-shingling his roof, fell and damaged his occipital lobe. When he came to, he was perfectly fine with one simple change:

DAVIS. He was scared of heights.

DR. DRISCOLL. All men were created equal, Mr. Tallison. He no longer hated or discriminated on the basis of color. And through years of tests we found that we can successfully end racial bigotry if we can just replicate this brain damage.

DAVIS. Okay. Let's. First of all, I am not a racist. This is more of a formality. For my job.

DR. DRISCOLL. Okay.

DAVIS. Sure. I mean, what, I'm intelligent, I understand that everyone has an inkling of, I mean — *you*, right, a little?

DR. DRISCOLL. No.

DAVIS. Exactly, me either! Hell, I run an urban shoe company.

DR. DRISCOLL. Urban?

DAVIS. It's a euphemism for African American. The point is, I spend a lot of time with African Americans. I know the African American culture and sell to the African Americans a product —

DR. DRISCOLL. You don't have to say "African American" every time, Mr. Tallison. You can simply use …

DAVIS. Urban?

DR. DRISCOLL. I was gonna say "a pronoun."

DAVIS. Oh. Well, I sell basketball shoes to *them*.

DR. DRISCOLL. Well, now the pronoun's offensive.

DAVIS. My overall point is, I don't think I'm a racist.

DR. DRISCOLL. Of course you don't. That's precisely why you are one. Do you understand?

DAVIS. No.

DR. DRISCOLL. We have a saying at the office, Mr. Tallison, that I think will appeal to you: "One who thinks, is. One who does not think, is. But one who is not one, thinks he is. One."

DAVIS. I don't understand a word you just said.

DR. DRISCOLL. You've proven my point perfectly.

DAVIS. I know what you're doing. Okay? I'm in marketing too. You sell the disease to sell the cure.

DR. DRISCOLL. Do you feel you need to be cured of something?

DAVIS. *(Annoyed.)* Listen: My dad was a salesman. My grandfather was a salesman. I'm a salesman. That's all I know and, frankly, all I care about. For the first time, I have a chance to succeed at a level they never could. And I won't let that be taken away because of some silly rules about what you can and can't say. I take this pill, the board is happy, and I run the company again! That's why I am here. So, write me a script and I'll get out of your hair.

DR. DRISCOLL. That's not how it works. I need to know you need it.

DAVIS. You just told me I needed it.

DR. DRISCOLL. For legal reasons, I need to hear it from you.

DAVIS. *(Beat, sighs.)* Fine. I was on the subway today. I don't usually ride the subway, but today I did. And these kids come in. They were … urban kids. And they were being very loud. Laughing and shouting. As if they wanted the entire subway to know they were having a good time. And all I could think was, "Jesus, are all black people this loud?" *(Beat.)* So, what do you think?

DR. DRISCOLL. What else you got?

DAVIS. How racist do I have to be?

DR. DRISCOLL. We like to cover our bases.

DAVIS. *(Considers.)* Okay. It's possible I may have ... exploited the murder of a young black teenager to sell more shoes. *(Driscoll stares, blankly.)* What?

DR. DRISCOLL. No, nothing, that's just *really racist.*

DAVIS. Okay, you know what...!

DR. DRISCOLL. No, please, it's good!

DAVIS. You know, I don't know how appealing brain damage sounds ...

DR. DRISCOLL. I assure you, it's perfectly safe.

DAVIS. Are there side effects I should know about?

DR. DRISCOLL. Different people react differently. Like any drug. Which is exactly why we conduct these little interviews. But I wouldn't worry. You seem like just the right kind of racist.

DAVIS. Thanks. *(He hands him a blue bottle of pills. Lights out.)*

Scene 11

A quiet corner of the Sky Max party. Signs up all over that say: "Sky Max 16" and "'Sup Now?"

Thomas drinks alone at the bar. Andie, a little tipsy, sits a few seats down.

ANDIE. *(Pause.)* I love these things. *(Nothing.)* I'm kidding. I don't really love these things. I was being ironical.

THOMAS. Yeah, I know. I love irony.

ANDIE. Oh. Aha. Now you're being ironical.

THOMAS. You like that word.

ANDIE. It was my Dictionary.com word of the day. I try to use it at least once.

THOMAS. Good, so you're done then. *(Slighted, she turns back to her drink. And then ...)*

ANDIE. Pretty ugly shoe, huh? *(Now she has Thomas' attention.)* I mean, I wouldn't wear those things on a bet, much less shoot someone for them. *(Whispers conspiratorially.)* It's okay, I can say that. I know someone who kinda works for the company.

THOMAS. Must be nice.

ANDIE. Right? I guess it's like how if you're Jewish you can make fun of Jews and it's funny, but if you're not, it's offensive.

THOMAS. Are you Jewish?

ANDIE. Me?? No! But I had this friend in college who was always using the word "retarded." "This is retarded, that's retarded, what a retard"? Even made jokes about retarded people; impressions, the whole thing. You know how retarded people have that voice? That like deaf person voice?

THOMAS. *(Uncomfortable.)* Uh-huh …

ANDIE. Well, he would do that.

THOMAS. What a talent.

ANDIE. Right? So, finally I said, "Look, maybe you should cool it on the whole retarded thing. It's kind of offensive to retarded people."

THOMAS. Not to mention the deaf.

ANDIE. Yeah, but they can't hear it. So then he says, "No, it's cool, my brother and my aunt are retarded. I can make fun of retards all I want!"

THOMAS. Sounds like he comes from a whole line of retarded people!

ANDIE. Right?! He's got like a free pass!

THOMAS. If he were Jewish, he'd have endless material!

ANDIE. He is Jewish!

THOMAS. Well, there you go!

ANDIE. Makes fun of Jewish people all the time!

THOMAS. What a comic genius!

ANDIE. He is funny. *(Beat.)* Like you can pretty much make fun of anyone you want.

THOMAS. *(Interested in this, humoring.)* Is that so?

ANDIE. Oh yeah! African Americans? God.

THOMAS. Didn't realize I had such a cultural advantage.

ANDIE. Are you kidding? You can make fun of anyone! Well, except for Native Americans but they're not that funny anyway.

THOMAS. No.

ANDIE. I mean, their names.

THOMAS. Their names are hilarious. *(Andie stops, as if realizing …)*

ANDIE. I'm offending you.

THOMAS. Don't worry about it.

ANDIE. No, I'm sorry, I do that sometimes, I think. I say things and people suddenly tell me I've said something I shouldn't have said and then —

THOMAS. No, stop apologizing. Really. You haven't offended me.

ANDIE. Oh. Good.

THOMAS. Can't speak for Jews or retarded Native Americans but ... actually, I find your honesty refreshing. You know, for a cracker bitch. *(She laughs, shocked.)* It's okay, I can say that. Our cleaning lady was a cracker bitch.

ANDIE. Yeah, well, you can say whatever you want, you're African American!

THOMAS. *(Mocking her whiteness.)* I certainly am African American!

ANDIE. I don't sound like that!

THOMAS. That is exactly how you sound.

ANDIE. Shut up!

THOMAS. "Oh my God! Shut up!"

ANDIE. *(Laughing.)* Stop! *(Smiles, beat.)* So, why are you back here alone? All broody and disconsolate.

THOMAS. Dictionary.com?

ANDIE. That obvious?

THOMAS. Inimitably.

ANDIE. What's that mean?

THOMAS. Check your inbox. *(Andie scoots closer.)*

ANDIE. So, are you like one of those angry black men?

THOMAS. *(Incredulous laughter.)* What?! Girl, seriously, you better be careful! Some of the shit you say...?

ANDIE. What?

THOMAS. I'm just saying, some of the things you say ... you should consider your audience.

ANDIE. You're my audience.

THOMAS. Yeah, well, you don't know me. You can't just say the things you say to a complete stranger. Jewish people and blacks and shit like that — there are consequences. You have to be responsible for the things that come out of your — *(Change of subject, tone.)* — and what if I am angry? Huh? Does my anger deserve your condescension?

ANDIE. I wasn't condescending you; I was just asking.

THOMAS. No. You said "angry black man." Like my anger only exists in a stereotype. That's condescending. I mean, does it occur to you that I might have something to be angry about? A reason that has nothing to do with my being black?

ANDIE. You're right. I'm sorry. *(Beat.)* Someone accused me of being too *white* today, so do with that what you will. *(Thomas starts laughing.)* Is that funny?

THOMAS. I've known you five minutes, you're the whitest chick I ever met.

ANDIE. Thanks. Maybe you guys should hang out. *(Beat.)* So, what are you angry about?

THOMAS. Maybe that's private.

ANDIE. Well, then what are you doing at a party?

THOMAS. I was expecting to see someone here tonight.

ANDIE. *(Teasing.)* A girl??

THOMAS. No. A guy.

ANDIE. *(Assuming he's gay.)* Oh.

THOMAS. *(Realizing.)* No!

ANDIE. No?

THOMAS. No.

ANDIE. Oh.

THOMAS. I mean, a man — a *dude* I've never met! He's supposed to be here tonight. All I got is his name.

ANDIE. What is it? Maybe I know him. *(Before Thomas can say, Davis enters.)*

DAVIS. Thomas! There you are! Where have you been?

THOMAS. Oh, I was just …

DAVIS. How was the funeral? Your family? Everyone okay? *(Thomas is taken off-guard by his effusive behavior.)*

THOMAS. Uh. Yes. Thanks for the flowers. It was very thoughtful.

ANDIE. I'm sorry; did someone die?

THOMAS. Oh, this is … I'm sorry, I don't …

ANDIE. Andie.

THOMAS. Andie. Andie this is Davis Tallison. The president of Sky. Andie was just telling me how much she loves the 16.

DAVIS. Well, I'm just the suit. It's all Thomas' design.

ANDIE. *Your* design? *(Thomas smiles.)*

DAVIS. He didn't tell you?

THOMAS. I was hoping to keep it a surprise. Hey, what are those Nike guys doing here? *(Davis looks. Then he bluffs.)*

DAVIS. What do you think? Taking notes. *(Changing the subject.)* So, do you work for the company? *(Andie is still flustered, and Thomas loves it.)*

ANDIE. Me? No. My fiancé writes your commercials.

THOMAS. *(Thomas' smile drops.)* Peter Trammel?

ANDIE. You know him? He was supposed to be here tonight, but I think he ditched me.

DAVIS. Probably for the best. Thomas wasn't the biggest fan of the 16 spot. *(Tense beat. Thomas and Andie stare at each other.)* Okay. Well, I gotta run. Come over when you have a minute?

THOMAS. *(Still staring at Andie.)* Sure.

DAVIS. Nice meeting you.

ANDIE. *(Still staring at Thomas.)* You too. *(Davis exits.)* I don't really think they're ugly, like in a bad way. They're probably very nice with the right pants! God, you just let me talk.

THOMAS. Peter Trammel. That's your fiancé?

ANDIE. You know him?

THOMAS. He the one thinks you're too white?

ANDIE. Yeah.

THOMAS. Marrying a black dude?

ANDIE. Peter? Yeah, he wishes he was black!

THOMAS. He's white?! The guy who wrote the 16 ad?

ANDIE. Yeah. Why?

THOMAS. *(Chuckles to himself.)* How ironical.

ANDIE. Look, you have to let me make it up to you. Let me buy you a drink. Okay? Please.

THOMAS. *(Considers.)* Sure. *(She turns to the bar, but he stops her.)* You kidding? Drinks here are free. Let's get outta here.

ANDIE. *(Blushing.)* Okay. *(Thomas takes her hand and they exit together.)*

THOMAS. *(Offstage.)* Oh, wait a minute — *(Thomas reenters to grab his hat. He turns to exit and bumps right into — Peter, who rushes in!)* Shit, sorry man — !

PETER. — Oh, God, no! I'm sorry! I'm such an idiot — !

THOMAS. It's cool, it's cool. *(Thomas exits as Peter shakes off his guilt, looks around for Andie. Lights out.)*

Scene 12

Davis' apartment. Late night. There's someone in the shadows, lurking around, singing to himself. Davis enters holding a baseball bat. He turns on a light to reveal Frederick Douglass. The hair, the beard, the whole thing.

DAVIS. *(Startled.)* AH!!

FREDERICK. SHHH! Damn! Wanna wake the whole neighborhood!?

DAVIS. Who are you?! How the hell'd you get in here?!

FREDERICK. You know who I am, shit!

DAVIS. *(Beat.)* I do?

FREDERICK. You sure as shit better!

DAVIS. *(Thinks.)* My high school principal, Lani Bishop??

FREDERICK. Man, I ain't no Lani Bishop! I'm Frederick Douglass!

DAVIS. *(Beat.) The* Frederick Douglass?

FREDERICK. Bingo mothahfuckah!

DAVIS. I don't understand.

FREDERICK. You're on drugs, bitch! I'm just a side-effect!

DAVIS. Driscotol.

FREDERICK. Ain't that some shit. *(Awkward pause.)*

DAVIS. Right. So. Can I help you?

FREDERICK. You got somethin' to eat up in this mug?

DAVIS. Uh. I have some left over salmon. And risotto.

FREDERICK. I'll take it. *(Davis pulls it out and Frederick begins eating. Davis watches awkwardly.)*

DAVIS. Well, I'd just like to say, I really respect what you've done for your people. I mean that. Quite an accomplishment.

FREDERICK. Oh yeah? What did you think of my books?

DAVIS. Your books. Yes. Well, I didn't read them all.

FREDERICK. Which one did you read?

DAVIS. Which one? Uh, I think it was the ... slavery one.

FREDERICK. Nigga, you didn't read a mothahfuckin' word!

DAVIS. You really developed a potty mouth, didn't you?

FREDERICK. Damn bitch! *Narrative of the Life of Frederick*

Douglass is only 75 mothahfuckin' pages! No wonder you got me talking like this!

DAVIS. I'm sorry, how long does this side-effect last?

FREDERICK. Shut yo ass up! Now! We gots to *change* some shit!

DAVIS. The honey glaze is too much, I know.

FREDERICK. Nah, nigga! I mean *real* shit! You have some power now! It's time to use it. Time to look at the world and say, "Shit, you ain't even close!"

DAVIS. Close to what?

FREDERICK. Being a country where people don't use the black man!

DAVIS. I don't use the black man.

FREDERICK. You don't use the black man?!

DAVIS. I don't think I use the black man.

FREDERICK. Motherfucker you use everyone! *(Re: the salmon.)* Damn, there is way too much honey glaze on this motherfucker!

DAVIS. What do you mean I use everyone?

FREDERICK. What do you think I mean, "Allen"!?

DAVIS. *(Catching the reference.)* My wife? I don't use her.

FREDERICK. Bitch offed herself five years ago and you still use that shit like Charmin! Anytime yo ass gets dirty, yo wife's suicide come clean you right up.

DAVIS. Jesus, that's really vivid.

FREDERICK. What, you think 'cuz you had some pain in yo life, gives you a right to be a racist?!

DAVIS. No, I just …

FREDERICK. I'm no math whiz, but I don't think one sad little white bitch equals an entire century of oppression, Allen. Do you?

DAVIS. I tried to help her. I did. She just, she wouldn't get better. No matter what I did, she just wouldn't get well!

FREDERICK. *(Snaps fingers.)* Hey! Focus Allen! These is white people problems!

DAVIS. Black people don't get clinically depressed?

FREDERICK. Hell, no! Now! Tonight at the party! Those Nike guys wasn't there to just suck yo dick and leave now was they?

DAVIS. No, they wasn't. *Weren't.* They wanna see the 17s. If our numbers are good and they like the new design, they're going to buy us out.

FREDERICK. And after Nike buys this bitch, you'll be selling each shoe with a Josh Groban Christmas album! But this shit was the plan all along, wasn't it? Water down the black culture 'til it melts into a creamy whiteness!

DAVIS. I wouldn't say a creamy whiteness.

FREDERICK. And you don't use the black man! Shit, I don't even wanna talk about Thomas' cousin. That's some sorry ass shit right there!

DAVIS. *(Suddenly realizing.)* I used his shit like Charmin, didn't I?

FREDERICK. Damn skippy.

DAVIS. My God … you're right.

FREDERICK. No shit, I'm right! I'm Frederick mothahfuckin' Douglass!

DAVIS. I'm using the black man!

FREDERICK. Good mo'ning, bitch!

DAVIS. It's like a whole new brand a slavery!

FREDERICK. Uh-huh.

DAVIS. Except this time it's American consumerism! MTV! Microwave popcorn. It's Orville fuckin' Redenbacher!!

FREDERICK. You know he lynched some mothafuckahs in his time!

DAVIS. Whoever owns the media owns the country!

FREDERICK. And it ain't no black man writing for yo shoes.

DAVIS. No! It's this one creamy white son of a bitch!

FREDERICK. Now you got white boys shooting each other for our kicks?!

DAVIS. That's fucked up!!

FREDERICK. It's an insult! I heard some Jewish kid on the Upper West Side, nicknamed J-Fresh, shot hisself for his own damn pair!

DAVIS. Well, to be fair, he was also retarded.

FREDERICK. Mentally handicapped.

DAVIS. Good call.

FREDERICK. It's one thing to take the blues and turn it into rock and roll. That's respect. But this shit?!

DAVIS. It's time for a change!!

FREDERICK. A-Men!!

DAVIS. Damn!

FREDERICK. Shit!

DAVIS. Bitch!

FREDERICK. Motherfucker!

DAVIS. How's the risotto?!

FREDERICK. DRY AS SHIT!

DAVIS. FUCK!! *(Awkward beat.)*

FREDERICK. Alright. I gotta run. Read the fuckin' crib notes next time, so I don't sound like no white man tryin' to sound like some fuckin' gang-bangin' mothahfuckah. I'ma take this. *(Takes the salmon.)* Peace, brother.
DAVIS. Good night, biznitch. *(Lights out.)*

Scene 13

Peter on his cell phone.

PETER. *(Nervous, leaving a message.)* Hello! Dr. Hodge. Emilia. Dr. Emilia. Hodge. This is Peter. I just wanted to call and apologize if I said anything the other day that made you … Anyway, just confirming I'll be there Thursday! And so. It's confirmed and all set. Officially. Okay. Alright. I'll see you then. Cool. *(He hangs up, embarrassed. Lights up on Andie in bed, reading* US Weekly *and speaking to someone offstage, like her first scene.)*
ANDIE. So, after all that, my therapist puts me under hypnosis and it turns out I was totally wrong about the being-molested thing. Which, I have to admit, was a little disappointing. I mean, you put that much emotional energy into anything it's exhausting, but to not have it pay off … He did get me to remember that I once walked in on my parents naked in bed discussing an episode of *M*A*S*H.* *(Thomas emerges from the bathroom, shirtless. He approaches the bed.)* I'm sorry, I'm talking a lot, I know. I've never done this before, and I mean … God, you're very attractive, aren't you? Oh. Okay; we're doing this again, I see. Well, oh. How nice. *(Thomas kisses her.)*
THOMAS. God, you are so white. *(They lay back in bed as the lights slowly fade out.)*

Scene 14

Emilia's office. Peter stands across from Emilia, who sits.

PETER. "The most monstrous monster is the monster with noble feelings." *(Beat.)* It's a quote that's been haunting me lately. Faulkner.
EMILIA. Dostoevsky.
PETER. I was close. I knew it was someone I'd never read.
EMILIA. And what does that mean to you?
PETER. You're the therapist.
EMILIA. I'm not the one haunted by it.
PETER. Are you angry with me?
EMILIA. Why would I be angry with you?
PETER. I don't know. Forget it. *(A moment.)*
EMILIA. I think it's easy. He wrote that to describe a character or a thing or an action — Not for us a hundred years later to apply it to ourselves however we please. Words are not islands. They're connected to sentences, which are connected to stories and ideas. To take words out of the pyramid of meaning, out of context, is ignorant. Irresponsible.
PETER. Like my job! I take a reference from one thing — a movie, a book, a painting — and I steal it to sell a bar of soap. I once stole a line from Sylvia Plath to sell a new contraceptive device. Client said it sounded too optimistic.
EMILIA. And "'Sup now?"
PETER. I heard it in a rap.
EMILIA. Do you like rap?
PETER. Sure, some. Actually, no. I find it violent and tasteless.
EMILIA. But you used it.
PETER. They say we're selling to kids who listen to it and so I listen. I hear the phrase, "'Sup now?" Sounds urban. So I steal it and slap it on a sneaker ad.
EMILIA. Out of context.
PETER. Out of the pyramid of meaning, yes! No knowledge of the origin behind it. In fact, contempt.

EMILIA. And then you take the attitude, the very attitude you find so offensive in rap music, and attach it to this shoe.

PETER. Yes! Which is then taken out of context again just before shooting a kid for these very shoes. Is that not monstrous?

EMILIA. *(A calm breath, suppressing.)* It's not your fault.

PETER. I can't work. I'm paralyzed by that stupid commercial I wrote. And they play it over and over!

EMILIA. You should be proud. I understand sales have doubled.

PETER. Yeah, and now you have rich white kids shooting each other over them! I mean, doesn't that offend you???

EMILIA. *(Sincerely confused.)* Why would that offend *me*?

PETER. Because these are kids who can afford the shoes, ignorantly imitating the struggle African Americans actually experience!

EMILIA. Not all African Americans experience that, Peter.

PETER. No, but they're making a mockery of your plight.

EMILIA. My plight?

PETER. Yes! These are idiots! Oblivious to what they're imitating and why! Which is exactly what I was doing when I wrote that commercial!

EMILIA. Peter —

PETER. I don't know shit about the Congo!

EMILIA. I'm sorry?

PETER. I think you should know that.

EMILIA. Are you talking about Africa?

PETER. Africa, Syria, here; I don't know shit! This is my point — everything blends!

EMILIA. What do you mean? What blends?

PETER. The issues! The words! Everything I say is wrong. Every-thing that comes out of my mouth is offensive because what do I know of struggle? Nothing! I am untouched! Unscathed!

EMILIA. Peter, I think maybe we should —

PETER. I look at you, the last month I've been in here, and I think, "What you must think of me?"

EMILIA. Why me?

PETER. I spend a maximum effort avoiding the banalities of my life! To not tell you what I do in a day, what my fiancée talks about, what we eat!

EMILIA. Why would I care what you eat?

PETER. What we *listen* to! The time we spend discussing, God knows what! I even lied to you just now. "'Sup now?" I never heard it in a rap. It just sounds like something a black person would say! My ignorance, ultimately, do you see, is monstrous! *(Then quickly.)* Would you go to dinner with me? *(Regretting.)* I'm sorry, that was — would you?

EMILIA. I think our time is up.

PETER. Right. Of course. I'm sorry. I'm. God. What you must think. *(He exits. She sighs, relieved. Suddenly, a deep voice in the darkness.)*

VOICE IN THE DARKNESS. That was rude! Throwing out a paying Caucasian like that. *(A light reveals Abe Lincoln sitting in the corner. Hat, beard, and all.)*

EMILIA. Oh, no, not you again! *(She searches for her pills.)*

ABE. You don't look too good, doc. Something I can do? Hey! Did I mention that I freed the slaves? Yep, totally freed 'em! You know, lots a people did big things, invented coffee makers or signed some bill ... but I'll tell you what feels really nice. Telling people you FREED THE SLAVES! Man. And they say the first black president was Bill Clinton. *(He eyes her pruriently.)* Not sure how appropriate this is, but you've got a whole Condoleezza thing going on and it is smokin'!

EMILIA. Please go away.

ABE. Michelle Obama?

EMILIA. Why do you do this to me!

ABE. You tell me, you're the one taking a race pill!

EMILIA. I take it so I don't have to think about race!

ABE. Oh, c'mon, doc! It's okay to express a little pent-up rage. You're an oppressed people! Peoples. Is it people or peoples? I never know. It's like monies. When is it appropriate to use the plural there? *(He sees that she's ignoring him and pretends to feel faint.)* Whoa ...

EMILIA. What's wrong?

ABE. My head. I don't know. Suddenly ...

EMILIA. What?

ABE. My head, it's burning up. *(She feels his head.)*

EMILIA. You don't seem hot.

ABE. You sure? Because it feels a little like ... jungle fever! *(He tries to kiss her and she pushes him off. He chuckles, devilishly.)*

EMILIA. I am a therapist!

ABE. You're a black therapist. Totally different!

EMILIA. What does it matter that I'm black?! Things were fine before he showed up! I like my life! I like my job! Why doesn't this fucking pill work with him — !!

ABE. Okay, okay! Calm down. We're gonna get through this. Together. Breath in. Breath out. *(She does this.)* Breath out. Breath through, and in, and out and through and around and good. *(She's totally confused.)* Now ... what's that *adorable* little mantra you have?

EMILIA. "They're not white people. They're people with problems."

ABE. And problems have no color.

EMILIA. The strong help the weak!

ABE. And you are?!

EMILIA. The strong!

ABE. Good! *(She smiles.)* Now ... what's the deal with black people and wine bars?

EMILIA. Excuse me?

ABE. I never see them there! I mean, do they not drink wine? Or just object to the idea of a bar that doesn't serve liquor? Because I can actually get on board with that.

EMILIA. I go to wine bars.

ABE. No, I mean like real black people.

EMILIA. *(Suppressing anger.)* I want you out of my office. And if you wanna come back and see me, I suggest you make an appointment.

ABE. Fine. So sue me for trying to free one more black person! *(Lights out.)*

Scene 15

A subway car. Peter sits, staring out. The two black kids from before enter but this time speak much differently.

KID 1. No, no, no, that movie was brilliant!

KID 2. You liked it? Really? That guy at the end? It made no sense!

KID 1. You're not taking into account the character's moral ambiguity.

KID 2. Oh, here we go again!

KID 1. Look, if he is an atheist, like he says, then what makes him feel like he's doing anything wrong? What is immoral to a man who has no moral system? No God?

KID 2. That is so trite. Please. Moral standards are not defined by God, they're defined by man.

KID 1. Who in the absence of a God has no reason to act moral.

KID 2. Kindness. For his fellow man. How about that?

PETER. Excuse me …

KID 1. You just contradicted yourself.

PETER. Excuse me?

KID 2. No, I didn't. I am saying if there is no God, then there are still rules, of the human condition.

PETER. Excuse me?! I was overhearing your conversation. And, well, I find it very interesting.

KID 2. Okay?

PETER. Look, this is kind of strange but I see you're wearing Sky shoes. I actually work for their advertising company. If you take this card here to any Footlocker retailer they'll redeem it for one free pair. *(He hands it to Kid 1.)*

KID 2. You're giving us free shoes? Because you like what we said?

KID 1. Hey, don't question it. It's a very kind gesture.

KID 2. You're right. That's very kind of you. While you're at it, would you mind removing your watch and wallet, please?

PETER. Excuse me? *(Kid 2 pulls out a gun.)*

KID 2. How about pretty please, sir.

KID 1. See?! This is what I'm talking about!

KID 2. No, no, you can't use this as an example!

KID 1. This is a perfect example! You steal and don't feel wrong about it.

PETER. I'm sorry, are you serious?

KID 1. I'm afraid he is.

PETER. You're robbing me?

KID 1. This is so embarrassing.

KID 2. Will you please hurry up! My stop is coming.

PETER. Of course! Uh. Here. Just don't shoot.

KID 2. Shoot?! Listen to this. Just because I'm black he thinks I would shoot him!

PETER. No! Of course not! I was just, you know, with the gun and everything …

KID 2. Oh, I see how it is! A black man can't brandish a gun at someone in this country without people thinking he's a cold-blooded killer!

PETER. No! You're right!

KID 1. He is?

KID 2. I am?

PETER. Yes! An African American man should be able to, you know, bear arms at someone and not be stereotyped.

KID 2. Right. Exactly. See? Thank you.

KID 1. Well, that's a first.

KID 2. Alright. Well, thanks for the card and watch and everything.

PETER. You're welcome. Just let me know if you need anything else.

KID 2. We will.

PETER. Okay, take care! *(The kids get off the train. Peter's smile drops, and he crumbles onto the seat. Lights out.)*

Scene 16

Thomas' bedroom. Andie strokes his hair as he lies in her lap. Thomas seems relaxed for the first time.

ANDIE. Have you ever thought about wearing eyeliner?

THOMAS. What?!

ANDIE. It's not gay if that's what you're thinking.

THOMAS. It's not straight either!

ANDIE. A lot of celebrities are doing it now. I was reading this article the other day that said Johnny Depp and Leonardo DiCaprio wear eyeliner, and they're not gay.

THOMAS. They're gay enough.

ANDIE. C'mon, it'll be fun. Let's try it!

THOMAS. No way!

ANDIE. C'mon!! Don't be whiny. *(She grabs her purse from the ground and straddles him. She starts to apply it.)*

THOMAS. *(Half-laughing.)* Girl, don't you put that shit on me …

ANDIE. Now DON'T move …

THOMAS. Whoa — careful!

ANDIE. *(Laughing.)* I haven't even touched you yet! Don't be a baby!

THOMAS. I'm worried about being a blind baby! *(She starts applying again.)* A blind … gay baby. *(They both giggle. They kiss. And she continues to apply the eyeliner.)*

ANDIE. I was watching this shampoo commercial the other day. It had this woman taking a shower and having an orgasm while putting it in her hair. Have you seen this? It was so stupid. Of course, then I bought it. I mean, I know I'm not gonna have an orgasm, right? I don't care how deep-cleansing it is, or where it cleanses deeply, but I bought it on the off-chance because, I don't know, what's the difference, really, between any of them, and I might as well get the one that says it'll make me cum. *(Thomas turns cold.)*

THOMAS. Alright, stop.

ANDIE. I'm almost done with this first one —

THOMAS. C'mon — cut that shit out! *(He pushes her off and gets out of bed.)*

ANDIE. Uh. What's going on?

THOMAS. Do you talk to him the same way you talk to me?

ANDIE. Who — ?

THOMAS. Peter! You tell him the same things? Your therapist, your magazines, that one show with that one guy, and then come here and rehash the whole thing?

ANDIE. He doesn't really listen anymore. Everything with him has to be so *heavy*. But when I talk to you it's … easy. You know?

THOMAS. *(Bothered by this.)* No! No, I don't. You know what…? *(He begins putting his clothes on.)*

ANDIE. Where are you going?

THOMAS. You know, you talk and you talk, and you have no regard for what you're saying! None! No respect for your audience!

ANDIE. You're my audience.

THOMAS. Exactly! This is what I'm saying! You, you, you talk about celebrities and napkin rings like we're two regular people! We're not two regular people! I mean, shit, what makes you think I give a flying *fuck* about that shit! What makes you think I don't have more *important* things … things I *think* about. Heavy. *Profound* shit!

ANDIE. *(Beat.)* Is this a black thing?

THOMAS. Okay. See? This. No.

ANDIE. What?

THOMAS. You! Trying to suck all my *power* from me.

ANDIE. What power? How?!

THOMAS. By talking! By saying the things you say. Looking at me like that. Like I'm just a normal guy. By not acknowledging this!

ANDIE. What?!

THOMAS. THIS!

ANDIE. You're not making sense. What are you missing?

THOMAS. The guilt! Okay? The fucking white guilt!! Where is it??

44

ANDIE. Oh, Jesus. Not you too!

THOMAS. You have no idea, do you? You think you can just walk around saying whatever you want, and there will be no repercussions.

ANDIE. What am I saying that is so illegal?!

THOMAS. Why are you here? Huh? With me. Why!?

ANDIE. I like you.

THOMAS. Bullshit! I'm black! Plain and simple!

ANDIE. Well, that too.

THOMAS. What?

ANDIE. What?

THOMAS. You're here because I'm black?

ANDIE. In the beginning, sure, that was part of it.

THOMAS. WHAT?!

ANDIE. What!? You just said that's what it was!

THOMAS. But you're not supposed to *admit* it! You're supposed to get all defensive and be like ... "Uh, no, no, I'm color blind, I had a black friend once!" Shit like that!

ANDIE. But it's true. In the beginning, Peter was being so self-righteous, acting like the man of the people, calling me white and ... Then I saw you, and you were, of course, black ...

THOMAS. And...?

ANDIE. And then we started talking.

THOMAS. And that's it.

ANDIE. Pretty much. I actually don't have any black friends. Except Tshombe. But he's like *really* black, like from Zambia, so it doesn't really count.

THOMAS. *There!* Right *there!* You can't just *say* that shit!

ANDIE. Sorry! You're right! African American. *(He begins breathing heavily.)* Well, then explain it to me! I want to understand! I mean, if there's something I need to learn, something I'm missing, some secret code then ... Thomas? Are you okay?

THOMAS. I can't. This thing. I've done what I came to do.

ANDIE. What is that supposed to mean?

THOMAS. I mean it's over!

ANDIE. Thomas ... Thomas? Tell me what you want?

THOMAS. Stop saying that! Stop acting so innocent!!

ANDIE. I don't get it! One second you like how honest I am, the next you want me to feel bad because you're an oppressed peoples!

THOMAS. Peoples?! What the hell is a peoples?!

ANDIE. Look, I'm the one taking the risks here! Have you considered that? I'm engaged! For the last month I've been creating different reasons for working late, inventing errands on the weekends. You want me to feel guilty for something — try *that*! That's *my* guilt. That I fell for you. And until a minute ago, I thought you were falling for me! *(Then.)* And you wanna hear something else I'm probably not supposed to say?! Ready for this!? Your blackness?? Not that interesting!! *(Thomas looks totally thrown.)*

THOMAS. What?

ANDIE. That's right! I could take it or leave it! How you like that? In fact, if you were white, I'd still have sex with you!

THOMAS. You're crazy.

ANDIE. How is that for "stealing your power"? You could be Irish and I'd "tap that shit"! Polish! German! White Russian!

THOMAS. Alright …

ANDIE. Canadian!

THOMAS. You lie!

ANDIE. Yep! A white-ass, Canadian, Mounty motherfucker, and I'd ride that Canuck shit all night long, EHH?!!

THOMAS. *(Covering his ears.)* STOP IT!

ANDIE. Deal with it, Thomas! Your "blackness," while it might have turned my head, is now nothing more than a minor detail in all of "THIS"!

THOMAS. You're a crazy white lady.

ANDIE. I think I love you.

THOMAS. *(Beat.)* You're engaged.

ANDIE. I don't have to be. *(He looks at her, breathing harder now.)*

THOMAS. No, that's … not what this was.

ANDIE. What was it?

THOMAS. Revenge.

ANDIE. For what?!

THOMAS. Charley Cross!

ANDIE. Who the hell is Charley Cross?

THOMAS. I DON'T KNOW! *(Beat, chuckles sadly.)* I don't know. *(Beat.)* But when he looked at me like that, in his office … "my people, your people," talking about his death like it was another commercial … winking at me like I was just black enough to lend him the credibility and just white enough to let it all slide. I had to let him know! I had to make him feel something! And guilt is the only power I have!! *(He begins to hyperventilate. Andie goes to him.)*

46

ANDIE. Shh. Come here …
THOMAS. … It's like this … weight … on my chest …
ANDIE. Shh. Take a deep breath. That's it. Let it out. You're breathing too fast. In … out. That's it. Just keep breathing. In. Good. Out. *(Beat.)* Tell me what I need to do, Thomas. You want me to watch what I say? I will. I'll filter everything. You want me to acknowledge this? Okay. Guilt? I can do that. Just don't leave yet. Don't go and tell me what you want. *(Thomas turns to her, perhaps considering the offer, but then exits.)* Thomas! Thomas, wait! Don't go! *(Lights out.)*

Scene 17

Davis' office. It's late, dark. Davis sits on the floor, drinking alone. He's been there awhile. Thomas sneaks in, wearing a black hoodie and a bag over his shoulder. He begins stealthily looking around the room for something when …

DAVIS. They fired me, Thomas.
THOMAS. *(Startled.)* Shit!
DAVIS. 'Course you already knew that, didn't you?
THOMAS. Tallison?
DAVIS. Little advice: this day and age, a black man sneaking around at night like that could be misconstrued. I'm just saying.
THOMAS. What are you doing here — ?
DAVIS. I did everything they asked. Tried to be more sensitive, say the right things — you can ask Frederick Douglass! He says I'm using the black man. Fine. So, I killed the 16 ad.
THOMAS. You killed it?
DAVIS. And they killed me. So, congratulations, Thomas. You win.
THOMAS. I didn't have anything to do with —
DAVIS. *(Explodes.)* BULLSHIT! This is *all you*. So … 'Sup now, nigga?! *(Off his look.)* Oh. What? You don't like me using that word? Did I *steal* from you? Rob you of the one thing you have that's *yours*? A *word*? Yeah, well, Sky Shoes used to be yours too, didn't it? "A black shoe for black people." Guess we stole that too. Welcome to America! Welcome to creamy whiteness! *(Thomas turns to leave.)* I'M NOT FINISHED!

THOMAS. *(Almost pitiably.)* Yeah. I think you are. *(He turns to leave again but —)*

DAVIS. Came for these, didn't you!? *(Davis holds up the Sky Max 17 prototypes. Thomas reaches for them but Davis pulls them away.)*

THOMAS. Give 'em to me.

DAVIS. Where do you think they'll put the Swoosh? Hm? Over here?

THOMAS. They're mine.

DAVIS. Yours? Didn't you hear what I just said?

THOMAS. Give 'em to —

DAVIS. No, this is good! Let's think about this! What is yours? What does the black man, Thomas Hodge, have when all the dust has settled? Your history? Your so-called culture? Nope! Bought and sold years ago — just like ours. Watered down. Processed and paid for. Hell, your identity has been whittled down to nothing more than a, a, movie, a rap song — a fucking commercial about a basketball shoe! You want some truth? You are a *cliché*, Thomas! Borrowed from clichés that we created! So, reach for the sky, bitches! *(Thomas turns from him.)* But, hey, no; you have your pain, right? Your daily struggles? A black man in a hard white world? *Bullshit!* No one owns their own pain anymore! The second you use it for currency, it's lost forever. Trust me. So don't rely on your *pain* for your power. That guilt "your people" love to push on us is nothing more than an advertisement for a product you don't own anymore. *Nothing is yours. (Beat.)* Your cousin…? Far as I'm concerned, he's the only real thing in this world.

THOMAS. *(Beat.)* He wasn't my cousin.

DAVIS. What's that?

THOMAS. Charley Cross. The kid who was shot? Never met him before in my life.

DAVIS. *(Beat.)* Are you fucking with me?

THOMAS. Nope. *(Davis slumps. Thomas takes the shoes and exits.)*

DAVIS. *(Existential.)* Ain't that some shit. *(Lights out.)*

Scene 18

Emilia's office, late. She's working. There is a frantic knocking at the door.

EMILIA. Who is it?

PETER. *(Offstage.)* It's Peter! I need to talk to you!

EMILIA. It's late, Peter!

PETER. *(Offstage.)* I was mugged! *(She opens the door. Peter enters, disheveled, possibly drunk.)*

EMILIA. Are you okay?

PETER. Yeah, I'm fine. How are you?

EMILIA. Are you drunk?

PETER. Why won't you go out with me?

EMILIA. Excuse me?

PETER. I've been perfectly nice to you, haven't I? Shown you every courtesy?

EMILIA. Peter ...

PETER. And I'm trying to learn! Surely, you can see the effort I've made to show you that I'm willing to be taught! *(He approaches. She retreats.)*

EMILIA. Okay. I'd like you to leave now.

PETER. I don't deserve your condescension, do I?! I mean, it's *me*! *Peter!* I'm one of the good ones, remember?! Look, if it's about my fiancée — you don't have to worry. It's over between us. She totally doesn't get me.

EMILIA. Peter, you're not thinking straight. You don't mean what you're saying.

PETER. Which part? That I'm in love with you or that you're condescending?

EMILIA. You're not in love with me! You feel bad about what happened to that boy; it made you examine some things in your life: your fiancée, perhaps, your job; now you're sublimating.

PETER. Do you prefer the term "black" or "African American"?

EMILIA. What?

PETER. I never know what's more PC. You say one, it could be

49

viewed as insensitive; the other, a little contrived — right?

EMILIA. Peter, please leave before I stop accepting your insurance!

PETER. C'mon! One date! I promise, I'm very charming when I'm not in therapy. *(He reaches and she slaps him away.)* Ah! What?! What is wrong with me!??!? *(Emilia is frightened.)* What more do I have to do?! Huh!? I *feel* for your *people*! Okay? The struggle? The, the *plight*?! Every week I come to you, contrite! And out there, all the time, in different ways! I am sorry! Okay?! I AM SORRY FOR MY PEOPLE! They *suck*! Whatever they did, whenever they did it, I renounce them! THEY ARE RENOUNCED! Jesus! I'm tired of paying for shit I didn't do! Slavery! Oppression! Forty acres and the Jim Croce Laws! I didn't bring you people over here! *(Beat.)* So, I see these black kids on the subway. They look a little sketchy and I think, "Hey, maybe I should go to the other side of the train" — but no! Because then I say to myself, "Who are you to judge?! They're probably very smart, educated kids! Who am I to assume that just because they're African American, they don't read Sartre?!" But guess what?! They pulled a *fucking gun* on me anyway! It didn't matter what I thought! So fuck them! And fuck *guilt*! I'm tired of it!! Watching my tongue, policing every syllable that comes out of my mouth! So, do me a favor, will you? Tell every black person or African American that you know — it wasn't me! Can you do that? Vouch for me?! Huh? IT! WASN'T! ME! *(He has her backed against the wall, shaking. He then relents; steps back, takes a deep breath.)* Whoa. That felt really good. Was that a *breakthrough*? Is that what they call it or whatever? I'm sorry if I scared you — did I? Jesus, that was amazing! Well … I guess I should probably go. Thank you. *(Peter turns to the door.)*

EMILIA. And Charley Cross? Are you sorry for him too?

PETER. Who?

EMILIA. That's funny. I thought that was the entire reason you were in therapy. A 14-year-old African American boy shot in the face because of a commercial. *(Beat.)* Imagine me listening to a man apologize over and over without the first clue as to what he's sorry for. He thinks it's because he's white. Well. Isn't that a shame. Even his contrition is out of context. His shame, ignorant and irresponsible. *(Beat.)* This was never therapy. It was a confession. To the only black person you know. And you thought if we went out, if you charmed me and we connected as people it would somehow magically pardon you of all wrong-doing. An instant hall pass that would walk you past every negro you meet with a fist bump. *(Emilia pulls out the bottle of Driscotol. She swallows a few and approaches him. He retreats.)* I come in here every day and listen to the problems of white folks. *Crackers* with *cracker* problems and *cracker* guilt!

PETER. Did you just say cracker?

EMILIA. I tell myself to be objective. Listen to the issues. Be understanding. "They're not white people," I say, "they're people with problems." But after a while it doesn't take. No matter how many pills I swallow, it doesn't suppress. Because the problem, Peter, is that I *do* understand. I too am unscathed. Untouched. Like you. So, I donate to the United Negro College Fund and I volunteer for NAACP. And I do it all to absolve myself. Out of guilt. Out of context. Just. Like. You. So, you see, you came to the wrong nigger for exoneration. You feel ashamed for your whiteness? So do I, Peter. So do I.

PETER. *(Pause.)* So, I should kind of go.

EMILIA. Not until you get what you came for.

PETER. What was that?

EMILIA. Absolution.

PETER. Really? I feel like we made a lot of progress today.

EMILIA. A few minutes ago, you were gonna leave your fiancée for me. *(She approaches again. He retreats.)*

PETER. I was subjugating —

EMILIA. Sublimating.

PETER. Sublimating. And I think I thought about it, what you said, and it makes sense, so, thank you.

EMILIA. Am I not black enough for you anymore?

PETER. No! You're totally black enough! *(She forces Peter into the chair and straddles him.)*

EMILIA. Put your hand on my breast.

PETER. Am I being charged for this?

EMILIA. What, you're no longer attracted to the chocolate?

PETER. Yes! Sure! I like the chocolate! I'm just — I'm engaged!

EMILIA. Peter! I am offering you forgiveness for killing my cousin!

PETER. Your cousin!?

EMILIA. Now put your hand on my breast! *(He puts his hands on her breast.)* Call me a nigger.

PETER. I can't say the N-word!

EMILIA. Kiss me!

PETER. No!! And it's not the chocolate thing, I promise!

EMILIA. Barging in here, filled with all that righteous indignation! How I'd rejected you! And now you don't want me?

PETER. Look, if things were different ...

EMILIA. I don't want you, Peter. Any more than you want me. I do, however, want to help you. Now ... open your mouth.

PETER. I just wrote a commercial.

EMILIA. And I'm offering you forgiveness.

PETER. It was just a commercial.

EMILIA. Open. Your. Fucking. Mouth. *(He opens his mouth and she puts a pill on his tongue, like communion.)* That's a good boy. *(She takes one herself.)*

PETER. What will it do?

EMILIA. Cure us.

PETER. Of what?

EMILIA. Hatred. Anger. Righteous indignation. *(She pops another in his mouth.)*

PETER. I'm not a racist.

EMILIA. Sure you are; we all are.

PETER. Who says?

EMILIA. Everyone. The TV, the radio, Abraham Lincoln. It's the rhetoric of our times.

PETER. And this will fix me?

EMILIA. You tell me. Do you want to be absolved?

PETER. *(Pause.)* Yes.

EMILIA. Then open. Really. Wide. *(He opens his mouth and she dumps the bottle down his throat. Lights out.)*

Scene 19

A subway car. Thomas sits, holding the bag with the Sky Max 17s. The two black kids walk into the car.

KID 1. You gotta be kidding me with that shit. That movie was incredible!

KID 2. Nah, man, that ending was bullshit.

KID 1. It was real!

KID 2. You telling me that kid couldn't get away if he wanted? He was running like that retarded nigga from across the street.

KID 1. He's not retarded, he's got Tourette's Syndrome.

KID 2. I don't care what he's got, nigga runs like a retard.

KID 1. Whoa, whoa. We got company. *(They approach Thomas.)* Hey brother, you looking for something?

THOMAS. Me? No. Thanks.

KID 1. You sure? We got some good shit.

THOMAS. I don't do crack.

KID 2. Crack?! Do we look like crack dealers to you?!

THOMAS. No! You're right. My bad.

KID 1. *(Proud.)* We sell top of the line pharmaceuticals!

KID 2. Under the counter, over the counter and *through the woods*.

KID 1. And from what I can tell, you could use a little something.

THOMAS. Why do you say that?

KID 1. Two in the morning, sneaking out of the Sky Shoes office ...

KID 2. Is-sues.

THOMAS. How did you know I was — what issues?

KID 2. Panic attacks?

THOMAS. Huh?

KID 1. You get 'em? Accelerated heart rate, sweating, trembling ...

KID 2. Shortness of breath, nausea ...

KID 1. Abdominal stress? You know!

THOMAS. Uh, yeah, sometimes.

KID 2. Do you ever experience feelings of intense fear in response to ordinary situations?

KID 1. What about the sensation that you're trapped, the world is coming to an end, doom, gloom ...

KID 2. Helplessness, hopelessness, loss ...

KID 1. Loneliness, night sweats, nightmares ...

THOMAS. Not really.

KID 2. What about periods of weightlessness?

KID 1. Heaviness?

KID 2. Bloating?

KID 1. Whatever the opposite of bloating is?

THOMAS. Uh ...

KID 1. Have you ever felt as though a particular pain hurt more than it was supposed to?

KID 2. Or less?

KID 1. Or, strangely, exactly as it should?

THOMAS. I sometimes hyperventilate.

KID 1. Impossible.

THOMAS. Why?

KID 1 and KID 2. Black people don't hyperventilate.

KID 1. Stick out your tongue. *(He does.)* Uh-huh.

THOMAS. What is it?

KID 2. How's your erection?

THOMAS. Right now?

KID 1. Do you *have* one right now?

THOMAS. No!

KID 2. Then when you have one.

THOMAS. It's fine, I guess.

KID 1. Nigga, you wearin' eyeliner?!? *(Thomas covers up, embarrassed.)*

KID 2. What about feelings of conflict?

THOMAS. Sure.

KID 2. Am I black, am I white…?

THOMAS. Yes!

KID 1. Hate?

THOMAS. YES!

KID 1. Uh-huh. Who? Mother, father?

KID 2. Sister?

KID 1. Childhood friends…?

KID 2. … The ones you abandoned fifteen years ago?

KID 1. Your white girlfriend…?

KID 2. … The one you abandoned *three hours* ago?

KID 1. Guy who wrote a commercial that killed your cousin!

KID 2. Who wasn't your cousin.

THOMAS. Yes.

KID 1. The one you never even knew.

KID 2. But you made a flag from his corpse and sold a shoe!

THOMAS. Okay — yes! All of it! I hate them all!

KID 2. But you're tired of the hate!

THOMAS. YES!

KID 1. Tired of being tired of the hate!!

THOMAS. My God, yes!

KID 2. Well, you happen to be in luck, brother. 'Cuz we got some premium shit, fix you right up.

KID 1. Make you forget you was ever black.

KID 2. Make you forget you was ever white.

THOMAS. What is it?!

KID 2. Brand new. Just hit the market. *(He pulls out a blue bottle.)*

KID 1. Driscotol!

KID 2. Or, as we call it on the street — "*Bleach*."

THOMAS. Is it safe?

KID 2. Perfectly safe.

THOMAS. Is it addictive?

KID 1. How addictive is bliss, motherfucker?

KID 2. Just one pill a day and you'll be able to work without that sting in your side!

KID 1. Am I white, am I black, shit — am I a man?!

KID 2. And best of all, you can tap that white bitch up in yo crib, conflict free!

KID 1. *Guilt* free.

KID 2. *Revenge* free.

KID 1. But you should definitely take it with food.

KID 2. What we're offering you is *life* without *weight*.

KID 1. *Words* without *meaning*.

KID 2. *Text* without *subtext*!

KID 1. *Faith* without the *burden of God*!! *(Then.)* And all we ask in return … is that bag you holding.

THOMAS. This? You don't even know what's in here.

KID 2. Prototype for the Sky Max 17s.

KID 1. I'm thinkin' that's definitely somethin' I could put on eBay.

KID 2. C'mon man, what do you need it for? Prove you're black? Sky ain't even a black brand no more.

THOMAS. This shoe is.

KID 1. Oh yeah? And you don't want them to have it.

KID 2. Like Noah takin' his shit on the Ark before the big wave!

KID 1. That it? You think you're saving us?

THOMAS. No …

KID 1. I mean, shit, you ain't Dr. King 'cuz you made a basketball shoe for black folks.

THOMAS. It's something; it's pure.

KID 2. Like the Sky Max 16 was pure?

KID 1. Sky Max 15?

KID 2. 14? 13? 12? Nigga, ain't nothing pure in this world got a logo on it.

KID 1. You think working at a black shoe company made you one of us?

KID 2. You were never one of us and you never will be.

KID 1. But once you take this, you won't give a fuck who you are!

KID 2. And if you buy now, we'll even throw in some crack.

(Thomas looks at the bottle ... and slowly reaches for it.)

THOMAS. *(Quiet.)* I think ...

KID 2. What's that?

THOMAS. I think ...

KID 1. You think what motherfucker?

THOMAS. I think, maybe, I think ... thank you, but I think I'm okay.

KID 2. *(Frustrated.)* C'mon man! This was a waste a damn time!

KID 1. Yeah. Shit. See you 'round. Racist motherfucker. *(The kids exit. A sudden lightness comes over Thomas. He takes out the 17s from his bag. He breathes in the new leather smell. Then takes off his shoes and puts them on. Lights out.)*

Scene 20

Thomas' apartment. Andie sits on the bed staring at Thomas, who stands in the doorway wearing his new shoes.

THOMAS. Hey. *(Nothing.)* You're still here.

ANDIE. Yeah. *(Another moment.)*

THOMAS. It's funny. Ever since I left, all I could think of was that commercial. You know, the one where the woman's shampoo gives her an orgasm? And I thought, my God. An actress actually had to act that out. In front of people. And not smart people, but advertising people. Marketing people. Executives discussing her performance behind the camera. "More moaning, I think we need more moaning here, I don't believe our product is making her cum enough!" And it was nice. To think about something you had said. This stupid commercial, which has nothing to do with anything. So ... weightless. Subtextless. And I thought, this is Andie. This is what I feel when I'm with Andie.

ANDIE. That's good, right?

THOMAS. I want you only to talk to me.

ANDIE. You mean...?

THOMAS. *US Weekly*, who's dating who on what series, which Starbucks is better, and what your therapist thinks of your latest dream. All of it. Spare me nothing about your day. The whiteness of your week. Your irresponsible honesty. I want you to talk, I was wrong before, say the things you say; filter nothing. I just want you to say them only to me.

ANDIE. Okay.

THOMAS. *(Smiling.)* Okay?

ANDIE. Only you. *(She buries her head in his chest. He strokes her hair. The only two people left in the world. Lights dim on their frozen embrace. Suddenly, New Age-y music begins to play, as a spot shines on Dr. Driscoll. He addresses the audience, like a commercial.)*

DR. DRISCOLL. Hi. I'm Dr. Leonard Driscoll. Do you suffer from racism and bigotry and just hate it? Do you ever have thoughts that make you say to yourself, "Whoa. That was really racist. Glad I didn't say it out loud." Of course you do. Well, we have the answer: Driscotol. Just one tiny caplet a day and all those thoughts you thought you shouldn't think … will fade away. Driscotol has become the top selling pharmaceutical in the country — after Viagra — And is helping people all over the world. But hey, don't take it from me. *(Spot on Davis.)*

DAVIS. My name is Davis Tallison, recovering racist and former exploiter of the black race. Since taking Driscotol I'm not only more sensitive, I'm more employable. And now I'm not just a satisfied client … I'm Driscotol's new marketing director. *(Spot on Emilia.)*

EMILIA. I'm Dr. Emilia Hodge. I am a psychiatrist. With Driscotol, I am now able to be objective in my sessions and treat people, not white or black, Latino, Asian, South Asian, Middle Eastern, Native American, East Indian, European, or "other" … but simply people with problems. Which is why I prescribe Driscotol to all my patients.

DR. DRISCOLL. So, remember, if you're feeling like you might be, and chances are you're right, and even if you think you're not, because that kind of means you are — consider Driscotol. Isn't that right, Peter? *(Spot on Peter. He tries to talk but the words barely come out. Like he's about to say something but then changes his mind. Comes up with the right way to say it and retreats.)*

PETER. I … *We.* I mean! What I mean is … actually … let me rephrase that. The thing I wanna … without meaning to offend, or *upset* … What I mean to say … and I don't want to speak for everyone here … or anyone or upset … *someone*! My thought is …

And really, what is that? My *thoughts*? The words … my uh … my *words*?? … My … *(Happily, confident.)* Driscotol!

DR. DRISCOLL. Driscotol. For the racist inside of you. *(They all hold up a bottle.)*

ALL ACTORS. Inside of all of us! *(Blackout.)*

End of Play

PROPERTY LIST

Basketball
Colorful basketball sneakers: "Sky 16" and "Sky 17" models
Pills
Glass of water
Laptop
Wedding invitation worksheet
Business card
Map of human brain
Bottle of blue pills
Hat
Leftover salmon, risotto
Baseball bat
Cell phone
Gun
Watch
Wallet
Purse
Eyeliner
Bag
Bottle of liquor
Glass

SOUND EFFECTS

Commercial announcers
Tooth brushing, off
New Age music

NEW PLAYS

★ **MOTHERS AND SONS by Terrence McNally.** At turns funny and powerful, MOTHERS AND SONS portrays a woman who pays an unexpected visit to the New York apartment of her late son's partner, who is now married to another man and has a young son. Challenged to face how society has changed around her, generations collide as she revisits the past and begins to see the life her son might have led. "A resonant elegy for a ravaged generation." –NY Times. "A moving reflection on a changed America." –Chicago Tribune. [2M, 1W, 1 boy] ISBN: 978-0-8222-3183-7

★ **THE HEIR APPARENT by David Ives, adapted from Le Légataire Universel by Jean-François Regnard.** Paris, 1708. Eraste, a worthy though penniless young man, is in love with the fair Isabelle, but her forbidding mother, Madame Argante, will only let the two marry if Eraste can show he will inherit the estate of his rich but miserly Uncle Geronte. Unfortunately, old Geronte has also fallen for the fair Isabelle, and plans to marry her this very day and leave her everything in his will—separating the two young lovers forever. Eraste's wily servant Crispin jumps in, getting a couple of meddling relatives disinherited by impersonating them (one, a brash American, the other a French female country cousin)—only to have the old man kick off before his will is made! In a brilliant stroke, Crispin then impersonates the old man, dictating a will favorable to his master (and Crispin himself, of course)—only to find that rich Uncle Geronte isn't dead at all and is more than ever ready to marry Isabelle! The multiple strands of the plot are unraveled to great comic effect in the streaming rhyming couplets of French classical comedy, and everyone lives happily, and richly, ever after. [4M, 3W] ISBN: 978-0-8222-2808-0

★ **HANDLE WITH CARE by Jason Odell Williams.** Circumstances both hilarious and tragic bring together a young Israeli woman, who has little command of English, and a young American man, who has little command of romance. Is their inevitable love an accident…or is it destiny, generations in the making? "A hilarious and heart-warming romantic comedy." –NY Times. "Hilariously funny! Utterly charming, fearlessly adorable and a tiny bit magical." –Naples News. [2M, 2W] ISBN: 978-0-8222-3138-7

★ **LAST GAS by John Cariani.** Nat Paradis is a Red Sox-loving part-time dad who manages Paradis' Last Convenient Store, the last convenient place to get gas—or anything—before the Canadian border to the north and the North Maine Woods to the west. When an old flame returns to town, Nat gets a chance to rekindle a romance he gave up on years ago. But sparks fly as he's forced to choose between new love and old. "Peppered with poignant characters [and] sharp writing." –Portland Phoenix. "Very funny and surprisingly thought-provoking." –Portland Press Herald. [4M, 3W] ISBN: 978-0-8222-3232-2

DRAMATISTS PLAY SERVICE, INC.
440 Park Avenue South, New York, NY 10016 212-683-8960 Fax 212-213-1539
postmaster@dramatists.com www.dramatists.com

NEW PLAYS

★ **ACT ONE by James Lapine.** Growing up in an impoverished Bronx family and forced to drop out of school at age thirteen, Moss Hart dreamed of joining the glamorous world of the theater. Hart's famous memoir *Act One* plots his unlikely collaboration with the legendary playwright George S. Kaufman and his arrival on Broadway. Tony Award-winning writer and director James Lapine has adapted Act One for the stage, creating a funny, heartbreaking and suspenseful celebration of a playwright and his work. "…brims contagiously with the ineffable, irrational and irrefutable passion for that endangered religion called the Theater." –NY Times. "…wrought with abundant skill and empathy." –Time Out. [8M, 4W] ISBN: 978-0-8222-3217-9

★ **THE VEIL by Conor McPherson.** May 1822, rural Ireland. The defrocked Reverend Berkeley arrives at the crumbling former glory of Mount Prospect House to accompany a young woman to England. Seventeen-year-old Hannah is to be married off to a marquis in order to resolve the debts of her mother's estate. However, compelled by the strange voices that haunt his beautiful young charge and a fascination with the psychic current that pervades the house, Berkeley proposes a séance, the consequences of which are catastrophic. "…an effective mixture of dark comedy and suspense." –Telegraph (London). "A cracking fireside tale of haunting and decay." –Times (London). [3M, 5W] ISBN: 978-0-8222-3313-8

★ **AN OCTOROON by Branden Jacobs-Jenkins. Winner of the 2014 OBIE Award for Best New American Play.** Judge Peyton is dead and his plantation Terrebonne is in financial ruins. Peyton's handsome nephew George arrives as heir apparent and quickly falls in love with Zoe, a beautiful octoroon. But the evil overseer M'Closky has other plans—for both Terrebonne and Zoe. In 1859, a famous Irishman wrote this play about slavery in America. Now an American tries to write his own. "AN OCTOROON invites us to laugh loudly and easily at how naïve the old stereotypes now seem, until nothing seems funny at all." –NY Times [10M, 5W] ISBN: 978-0-8222-3226-1

★ **IVANOV translated and adapted by Curt Columbus.** In this fascinating early work by Anton Chekhov, we see the union of humor and pathos that would become his trademark. A restless man, Nicholai Ivanov struggles to dig himself out of debt and out of provincial boredom. When the local doctor, Lvov, informs Ivanov that his wife Anna is dying and accuses him of worsening her condition with his foul moods, Ivanov is sent into a downward spiral of depression and ennui. He soon finds himself drawn to a beautiful young woman, Sasha, full of hope and energy. Finding himself stuck between a romantic young mistress and his ailing wife, Ivanov falls deeper into crisis, heading toward inevitable tragedy. [8M, 8W] ISBN: 978-0-8222-3155-4

DRAMATISTS PLAY SERVICE, INC.
440 Park Avenue South, New York, NY 10016 212-683-8960 Fax 212-213-1539
postmaster@dramatists.com www.dramatists.com

NEW PLAYS

★ **I'LL EAT YOU LAST: A CHAT WITH SUE MENGERS by John Logan.** For more than 20 years, Sue Mengers' clients were the biggest names in show business: Barbra Streisand, Faye Dunaway, Burt Reynolds, Ali MacGraw, Gene Hackman, Cher, Candice Bergen, Ryan O'Neal, Nick Nolte, Mike Nichols, Gore Vidal, Bob Fosse…If her clients were the talk of the town, she was the town, and her dinner parties were the envy of Hollywood. Now, you're invited into her glamorous Beverly Hills home for an evening of dish, dirty secrets and all the inside showbiz details only Sue can tell you. "A delectable soufflé of a solo show…thanks to the buoyant, witty writing of Mr. Logan" –NY Times. "80 irresistible minutes of primo tinseltown dish from a certified master chef." –Hollywood Reporter. [1W] ISBN: 978-0-8222-3079-3

★ **PUNK ROCK by Simon Stephens.** In a private school outside of Manchester, England, a group of highly-articulate seventeen-year-olds flirt and posture their way through the day while preparing for their A-Level mock exams. With hormones raging and minimal adult supervision, the students must prepare for their future — and survive the savagery of high school. Inspired by playwright Simon Stephens' own experiences as a teacher, PUNK ROCK is an honest and unnerving chronicle of contemporary adolescence. "[A] tender, ferocious and frightning play." –NY Times. "[A] muscular little play that starts out funny and ferocious then reveals its compassion by degrees." –Hollywood Reporter. [5M, 3W] ISBN: 978-0-8222-3288-9

★ **THE COUNTRY HOUSE by Donald Margulies.** A brood of famous and longing-to-be-famous creative artists have gathered at their summer home during the Williamstown Theatre Festival. When the weekend takes an unexpected turn, everyone is forced to improvise, inciting a series of simmering jealousies, romantic outbursts, and passionate soul-searching. Both witty and compelling, THE COUNTRY HOUSE provides a piercing look at a family of performers coming to terms with the roles they play in each other's lives. "A valentine to the artists of the stage." –NY Times. "Remarkably candid and funny." –Variety. [3M, 3W] ISBN: 978-0-8222-3274-2

★ **OUR LADY OF KIBEHO by Katori Hall.** Based on real events, OUR LADY OF KIBEHO is an exploration of faith, doubt, and the power and consequences of both. In 1981, a village girl in Rwanda claims to see the Virgin Mary. Ostracized by her schoolmates and labeled disturbed, everyone refuses to believe, until impossible happenings appear again and again. Skepticism gives way to fear, and then to belief, causing upheaval in the school community and beyond. "Transfixing." –NY Times. "Hall's passionate play renews belief in what theater can do." –Time Out [7M, 8W, 1 boy] ISBN: 978-0-8222-3301-5

DRAMATISTS PLAY SERVICE, INC.
440 Park Avenue South, New York, NY 10016 212-683-8960 Fax 212-213-1539
postmaster@dramatists.com www.dramatists.com

NEW PLAYS

★ **AGES OF THE MOON by Sam Shepard.** Byron and Ames are old friends, reunited by mutual desperation. Over bourbon on ice, they sit, reflect and bicker until fifty years of love, friendship and rivalry are put to the test at the barrel of a gun. "A poignant and honest continuation of themes that have always been present in the work of one of this country's most important dramatists, here reconsidered in the light and shadow of time passed." –NY Times. "Finely wrought…as enjoyable and enlightening as a night spent stargazing." –Talkin' Broadway. [2M] ISBN: 978-0-8222-2462-4

★ **ALL THE WAY by Robert Schenkkan. Winner of the 2014 Tony Award for Best Play.** November, 1963. An assassin's bullet catapults Lyndon Baines Johnson into the presidency. A Shakespearean figure of towering ambition and appetite, this charismatic, conflicted Texan hurls himself into the passage of the Civil Rights Act—a tinderbox issue emblematic of a divided America—even as he campaigns for re-election in his own right, and the recognition he so desperately wants. In Pulitzer Prize and Tony Award–winning Robert Schenkkan's vivid dramatization of LBJ's first year in office, means versus ends plays out on the precipice of modern America. ALL THE WAY is a searing, enthralling exploration of the morality of power. It's not personal, it's just politics. "…action-packed, thoroughly gripping… jaw-dropping political drama." –Variety. "A theatrical coup…nonstop action. The suspense of a first-class thriller." –NY1. [17M, 3W] ISBN: 978-0-8222-3181-3

★ **CHOIR BOY by Tarell Alvin McCraney.** The Charles R. Drew Prep School for Boys is dedicated to the creation of strong, ethical black men. Pharus wants nothing more than to take his rightful place as leader of the school's legendary gospel choir. Can he find his way inside the hallowed halls of this institution if he sings in his own key? "[An] affecting and honest portrait…of a gay youth tentatively beginning to find the courage to let the truth about himself become known." –NY Times. "In his stirring and stylishly told drama, Tarell Alvin McCraney cannily explores race and sexuality and the graces and gravity of history." –NY Daily News. [7M] ISBN: 978-0-8222-3116-5

★ **THE ELECTRIC BABY by Stefanie Zadravec.** When Helen causes a car accident that kills a young man, a group of fractured souls cross paths and connect around a mysterious dying baby who glows like the moon. Folk tales and folklore weave throughout this magical story of sad endings, strange beginnings and the unlikely people that get you from one place to the next. "The imperceptible magic that pervades human existence and the power of myth to assuage sorrow are invoked by the playwright as she entwines the lives of strangers in THE ELECTRIC BABY, a touching drama." –NY Times. "As dazzling as the dialogue is dreamful." –Pittsburgh City Paper. [3M, 3W] ISBN: 978-0-8222-3011-3

DRAMATISTS PLAY SERVICE, INC.
440 Park Avenue South, New York, NY 10016 212-683-8960 Fax 212-213-1539
postmaster@dramatists.com www.dramatists.com